PIANO · VOCAL · GUITAR

THE DIMITRI TIOMKIN
ANTHOLOGY

Editors: Patrick Russ, Paul Henning, Warren Sherk

Special thanks to Olivia Tiomkin Douglas; Stephen Hanson, Ned Comstock,
and John Brockman with the Dimitri Tiomkin Collection at the USC Cinematic Arts Library.

For information about Dimitri Tiomkin's life, film scores and songs,
visit **www.dimitritiomkin.com**. To download high-quality mp3 recordings of
several of the songs included in this anthology, click on the Anthology link
on the home page and enter the password **Dimitri_mp3s**.

ISBN 978-1-4234-3778-9

7777 W. BLUEMOUND RD. P.O. BOX 13819 MILWAUKEE, WI 53213

Visit Hal Leonard Online at
www.halleonard.com

DIMITRI TIOMKIN (1894–1979)

One of Hollywood's most distinguished and best-loved film composers, Dimitri Tiomkin carved a prolific career as a songwriter as well as a composer of some of the most celebrated and iconic film scores of the Golden Age. Over five consecutive decades, Tiomkin received nearly two dozen Academy Award nominations for score and song. Of these, he took home four Oscars. Other honors include a commemorative postage stamp issued by the United States Postal Service as part of the Hollywood Composers series; a Maurice Ravel gold medal from SACEM, the French performing rights society; and recognition from the French and Spanish governments in the form of Officer of the National Order of the Legion of Honor and La Cruz de Caballero de la Orden de Isabel la Católica.

Dimitri Zinovich Tiomkin was born in Kremenchuk, Russia. The year of his birth often has been cited as 1899, as indicated on his passport. When Tiomkin emigrated from Russia to Germany in the early 1920s, his father, who had remarried and was living in Berlin, helped arrange for the travel papers. It is now believed that the elder Tiomkin shaved five years off his son's age in the official paperwork in an attempt to conceal his own true age from his second wife.

As a student of Alexander Glazunov at the St. Petersburg Conservatory, where Sergei Prokofiev was also enrolled, Tiomkin excelled as a solo pianist. He also taught piano. It was one of his students, an African-American minstrel-show singer from New Orleans, who first introduced Tiomkin to ragtime, blues, and early jazz, which fostered Tiomkin's interest in American popular music. Following the Russian revolution, Tiomkin left for Germany, where his appearance with the Berlin Philharmonic helped further his reputation as a concert pianist.

At the urging of his roommate and fellow pianist Michael Kariton, Tiomkin then moved to Paris to perform in programs featuring two pianos, which were fashionable at the time. Tiomkin's globe-trotting continued as he and Kariton sailed to New York in 1925 as accompanists to a ballet troupe headed by the Austrian-born ballerina and choreographer Albertina Rasch. The professional relationship between Tiomkin and Rasch grew personal, and they were married in 1927. He continued working as a pianist, performing the European premiere of Concerto in F by his friend George Gershwin and providing music accompaniment for Rasch's ballets, first in vaudeville, then in films.

The couple eventually settled in Hollywood, where Tiomkin pursued film work. He began by supplying orchestral music for musical films that included dance numbers conceived and choreographed by Rasch, whose name carried cachet due to her work on Broadway and her touring dance troupe, the Albertina Rasch Girls. From there, he went on to score more than 130 feature films in all genres, including *Lost Horizon*, *It's a Wonderful Life*, *The Thing*, and *The Guns of Navarone*. Tiomkin is closely associated with the Western genre because of his work on *High Noon* and *Giant*; the John Wayne films *Red River*, *Rio Bravo*, and *The Alamo*; and the quintessential theme from the television series *Rawhide*. Frank Capra (who was also a close friend), Howard Hawks, Alfred Hitchcock, and Fred Zinnemann are among the respected directors who called on his services. His collaborations with the producer Samuel Bronston resulted in the acclaimed scores for *55 Days at Peking* (1963), *The Fall of the Roman Empire* (1964), and *Circus World* (1964).

After Rasch died in 1967, Tiomkin returned to his native Russia to film *Tchaikovsky*, a pre-glasnost American-Russian coproduction. Tiomkin arranged the music and served as executive producer for the film, which was nominated for an Academy Award in the foreign language film category. In 1972, Tiomkin wed Olivia Cynthia Patch in London, and they maintained residences in London and Paris. In the twilight of his career, Dimi, as he was known to friends, enjoyed playing classical music at the piano. He died in London on November 11, 1979.

Part of Tiomkin's enduring legacy is his unerring gift for melody. "Do Not Forsake Me, Oh My Darlin'," the theme song for *High Noon* (1952), brought him enormous popularity and success and changed the course of his career. By incorporating a song with lyrics into his score for the film, Tiomkin bucked tradition and sparked a theme-song trend. He suddenly found himself in demand as a songwriter, particularly for main-title compositions that would capture the mood of a film. Over the next several years, Tiomkin wrote a title song or ballad for nearly every picture he scored, often working with lyricists Ned Washington or Paul Francis Webster. Together they racked up a number of Oscar-nominated songs: "Thee I Love" from *Friendly Persuasion*, the title song from *Wild Is the Wind*, "Strange Are the Ways of Love" from *The Young Land*, "The Green Leaves of Summer" from *The Alamo*, the title song from *Town Without Pity*, and "So Little Time" from *55 Days at Peking*. (All are included in this volume.)

Although it may appear that Tiomkin first burst onto the scene as a songwriter in the 1950s, he actually was writing songs as early as the 1920s. He composed a number of songs for the 1930s musical *Alice in Wonderland* and dabbled in several Broadway projects beginning in the late 1920s, a transitory period in which he was leaving behind his pianist roots and contemplating a career either in Hollywood or on Broadway. Three songs in this volume represent Tiomkin's work for stage musicals, and each offers a fascinating glimpse into the emerging songwriter. They are "I'll Ballyhoo You" from *A Little Racketeer* (1932), and two compositions from unproduced shows: "Rockette Song" from *The Big Time Revue*, and "Sweet Surrender," written for a musical of the same name during a slowdown in film production at the outset of World War II.

In the process of compiling this folio, some 200 songs were found to have been written by Tiomkin. Forty-eight of those were selected for this songbook; most are from films dating from 1952 to 1963, his golden years of film songdom. The earliest film song, "Headin' Home" from the 1946 Western *Duel in the Sun*, is a reflection of his artistic potential. It features a memorable melody set over a lilting bass line that mimics a folk guitar pattern typically found in what used to be called country and western music. Tiomkin was a natural when it came to writing songs for Westerns, and the diversity and quality of work he contributed to the genre is remarkable. Compare the anthemic "Giant (This Then Is Texas)" with the underlying rhythmic pulse of "Gunfight at the O.K. Corral," the haunting beauty of "The Green Leaves of Summer," and the tender, dreamy, and romantic strains of "Quand je rêve" from *The Big Sky*.

Tiomkin's songwriting talent, combined with his scoring expertise, led to evocative compositions that enhanced the drama in a film. He utilized the ballad, with its strong narrative and storytelling elements, to layer musical and lyrical commentary onto a scene. For instance, "Ballad of the Alamo" opens with a galloping rhythm of minor chords and the Paul Francis Webster lyrics, "In the southern part of Texas, near the town of San Antone, stands a fortress all in ruins that the weeds have overgrown." Other examples include the "Jett Rink Ballad" ("I'm just a ranch hand...") from *Giant*—which grew to be so closely identified with its star that it became known as the "James Dean Theme"—and "Ballad of the War Wagon."

On the heels of Tiomkin's success with "Do Not Forsake Me" came a quintet of songs that showcase the composer's versatility. "Love, Look What You've Done to Me" from the 1953 Alfred Hitchcock thriller *I Confess*, sports a jazz feel and shares similarities with "Love Like Ours" from *The Men* (1950), with its jazzlike chord progressions. "Julie," the romantic ode in *Take the High Ground*, is heard in that film as a song, as source music in a nightclub scene, and as dramatic underscore. In *Dial M for Murder*, a waltz melody in three-quarter time becomes the transfigured love song "My Favorite Memory," reworked in common time with extended harmonies. Finally, Tiomkin followed the uplifting theme from *The High and the Mighty* with the stately "Land of the Pharaohs."

Tiomkin's songs often touched the lives of those who heard or performed them. For some artists, their biggest hits were Tiomkin compositions: Pat Boone for "Thee I Love," Gene Pitney for "Town Without Pity," Johnny Mathis for "Wild Is the Wind," Frankie Laine for "Do Not Forsake Me." After *High Noon*, Laine became a frequent interpreter of Tiomkin's songs; he sang the title tune for *Strange Lady in Town*, for example. Nat "King" Cole covered the title song from *Return to Paradise* in a classic Nelson Riddle arrangement. Robert Merrill lent his voice to "Kashmir," a calypso ballad that recalls Tiomkin's Russian roots and was featured in *Search for Paradise*, the widescreen Cinerama Himalayan fantasy. Associating a famous voice with a song can help memorialize it in the minds and hearts of its viewing audience. In *Rio Bravo*, star Dean Martin crooned the title tune, and he and costar Ricky Nelson sang on screen "My Rifle, My Pony and Me." The affable James Stewart performs "Follow the River" in *Night Passage*.

There are other songs with which Tiomkin left his mark, such as "Never Be It Said" from *Champion*, starring Kirk Douglas as a prizefighter. For *Friendly Persuasion*, a Civil War drama with Gary Cooper, Tiomkin contributed a nostalgic dancelike tune called "Indiana Holiday." The folksy theme from Fred Zinnemann's 1960 film, *The Sundowners*, set in Australia, captures the feel of the great outdoors. In addition to the score, Tiomkin wrote a song with lyricist Frederick Herbert for *It's a Wonderful Life* that ultimately was not used in the film. With the advent of television came the enduring classic theme for *Rawhide* (1959), followed two years later by the theme for *Gunslinger*.

Thanks to his background as a classical pianist, Tiomkin's work is well suited to piano adaptation, particularly his music for epic films and large ensembles: the title song for *The Guns of Navarone*, the jaunty "John Wayne March" from *Circus World* (1964), and "The Fall of Love" from *The Fall of the Roman Empire* (1964), with its plaintive melody offset by chromatic counterpoint. Tiomkin's ability to switch between styles is evident in *55 Days at Peking*, which features both a martial title song and a lyrical love theme, "So Little Time." Two other themes that translate well into piano solos are the dreamy main title from *The Old Man and the Sea* (1958) and the love theme from *Lost Horizon* (1936). Surprisingly, there are not a lot of piano solos in Tiomkin's film scores. An exception is "Nostalgia," heard in the film noir melodrama *Angel Face* (1953).

Two specialty songs are bound to receive more attention with this publication. For the 1956 wedding of Prince Rainier of Monaco and the actress Grace Kelly, Tiomkin wrote "The Prince and Princess Wedding Waltz," also known as "The Grace Kelly Wedding Waltz." The actress, who had appeared in two Tiomkin-scored films, *Dial M for Murder* and *High Noon*, wrote in a letter to the composer that she would be honored to have a song written by him. The other specialty song, "The First Christmas," written for *Woman's Home Companion* magazine in 1953, is one of several holiday-themed songs penned by the composer. Singer Jill Corey's performance became the first commercial recording of her budding career.

Some of the works in this songbook, such as "First Christmas," "I'll Ballyhoo You," "The Need for Love" from *The Unforgiven*, "Wait for Love" from *Tension at Table Rock*, and the theme from *36 Hours*, are available for the first time since their initial publication. Other compositions, such as "Love Like Ours," are premier piano-vocal arrangements published here for the first time.

Symphonic orchestrator Patrick Russ, along with composer Paul Henning and myself, spent many hours selecting, preparing, arranging, and editing the songs for publication. We owe a debt of gratitude to Olivia Tiomkin Douglas for her unwavering support of the Tiomkin music catalog.

Those interested in learning more about the composer's life, film scores, and songs may consult his autobiography, *Please Don't Hate Me*, and Christopher Palmer's *Dimitri Tiomkin: A Portrait*, as well as visit www.dimitritiomkin.com.

Warren M. Sherk
Composer/music archivist

Contents

Chronological Contents (BY GENRE)

BALLAD OF THE ALAMO
from the 1960 Motion Picture THE ALAMO

Music by DIMITRI TIOMKIN
Words by PAUL WEBSTER

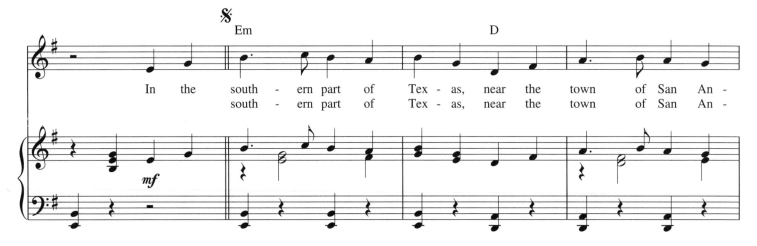

In the south - ern part of Tex - as, near the town of San An -
south - ern part of Tex - as, near the town of San An -

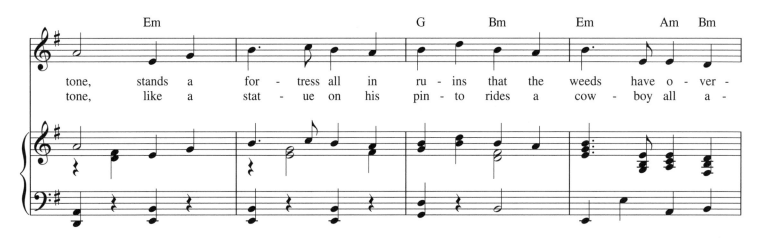

tone, stands a for - tress all in ru - ins that the weeds have o - ver
tone, like a stat - ue on his pin - to rides a cow - boy all a -

grown. _____ You may look in vain for cross - es and you'll
lone. _____ And he sees the cat - tle graz - ing where a

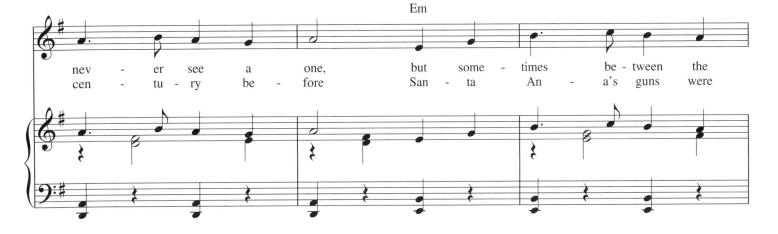

Em

never - er see a one, but some - times be - tween the
cen - tu - ry be - fore San - ta An - a's guns were

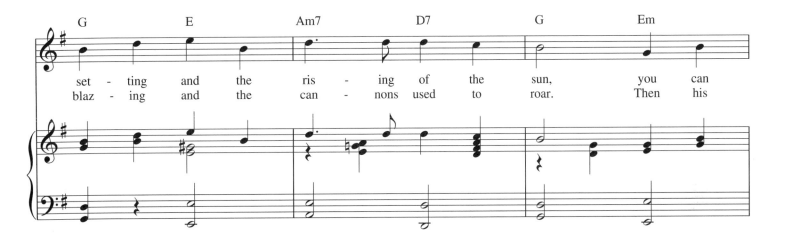

G   E   Am7   D7   G   Em

set - ting and the ris - ing of the sun, you can
blaz - ing and the can - nons used to roar. Then his

Am7   D7   G   Am7   D7   G   E7

hear a ghost - ly bu - gle as the men go march - ing by. You can
eyes turn sort - a mist - y and his men heart be - gins to glow, and he

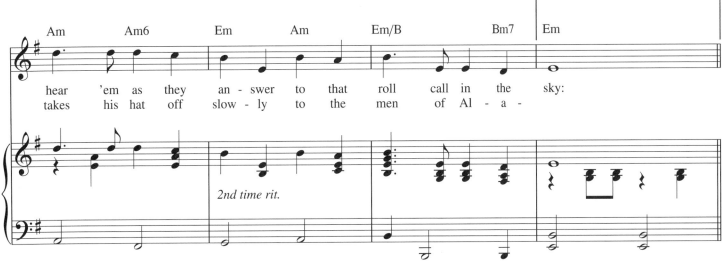

Am   Am6   Em   Am   Em/B   Bm7   Em

To Interlude

hear 'em as they an - swer to that roll call in the sky:
takes his hat off slow - ly to the men of Al - a -

2nd time rit.

Fine

Em · E7 · Am7 · D9 · Em/G · Am

mo, _____ to the thir - teen days of glo - ry at the

a tempo ma meno mosso · *f*

Tempo I

Em/B · Bm7 · Em

siege of Al - a - mo. _____

rit. · *rit. e dim.* · *p*

Interlude

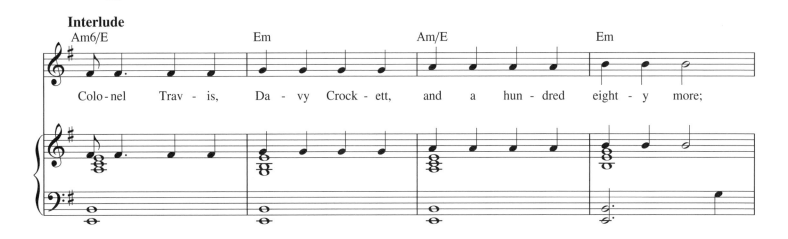

Am6/E · Em · Am/E · Em

Colo - nel Trav - is, Da - vy Crock - ett, and a hun - dred eigh - ty more;

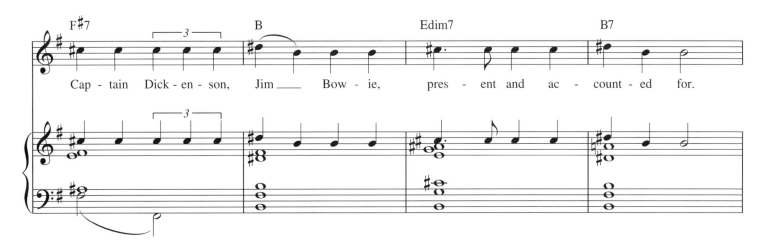

F#7 · B · Edim7 · B7

Cap - tain Dick - en - son, Jim ___ Bow - ie, pres - ent and ac - count - ed for.

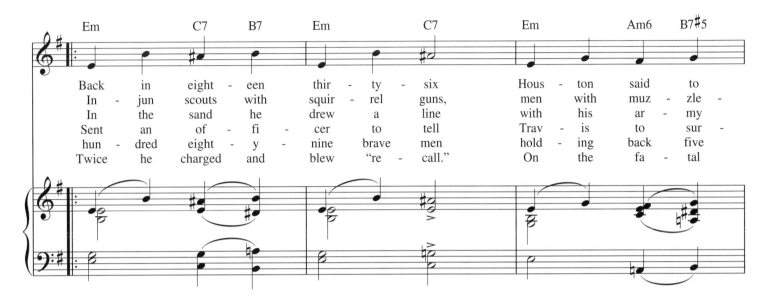

Back in eight - een thir - ty - six Hous - ton said to
In - jun scouts with squir - rel guns, men with muz - zle -
In the sand he drew a line with his ar - my
hun - dred eight - y - nine brave men hold - ing back five
Twice he charged and blew "re - call." On the fa - tal

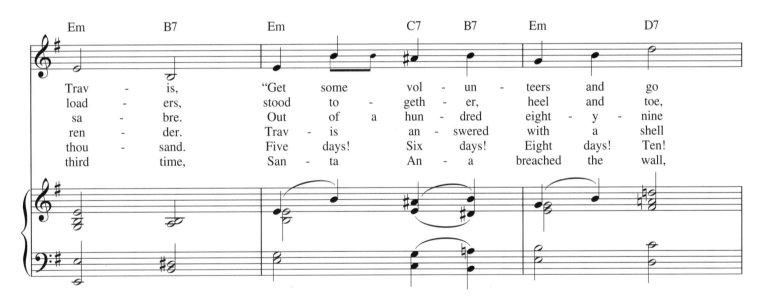

Trav - is, "Get some vol - un - teers and go
load - ers, stood to - geth - er, heel and toe,
sa - bre. Out of a hun - dred eight - y - nine
ren - der. Trav - is an - swered with a shell
thou - sand. Five days! Six days! Eight days! Ten!
third time, San - ta An - a breached the wall,

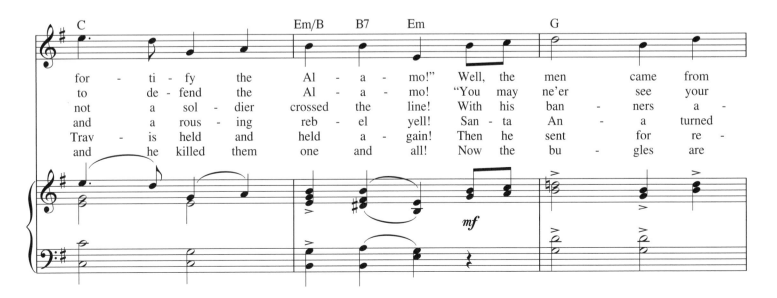

for - ti - fy the Al - a - mo!" Well, the men came from
to de - fend the Al - a - mo! "You may ne'er see your
not a sol - dier crossed the line! With his ban - ners a -
and a rous - ing reb - el yell! San - ta An - a turned
Trav - is held and held a - gain! Then he sent for re -
and he killed them one and all! Now the bu - gles are

A bugle call appealing to the enemy to "surrender or die."

THE FIRST CHRISTMAS

for a 1953 Issue of *Woman's Home Companion* Magazine

Words by NED WASHINGTON
Music by DIMITRI TIOMKIN
Arranged by Paul Henning
and Patrick Russ

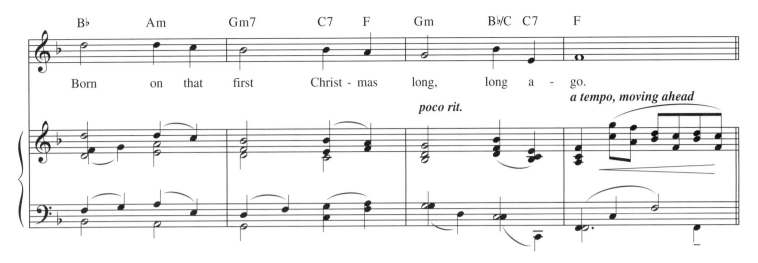

Born on that first Christ - mas long, long a - go.

poco rit.

a tempo, moving ahead

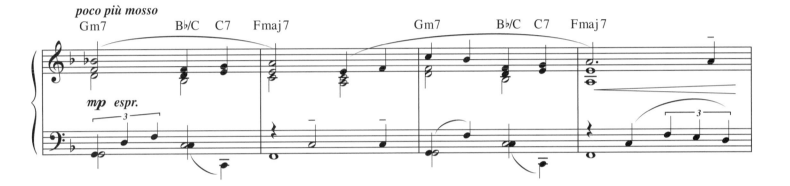

poco più mosso

mp espr.

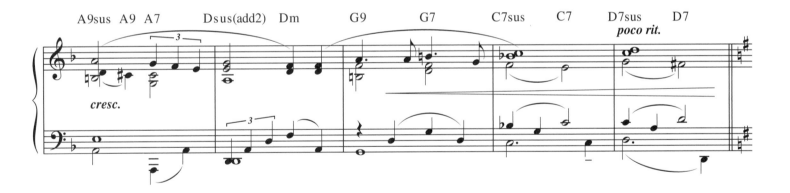

cresc.

poco rit.

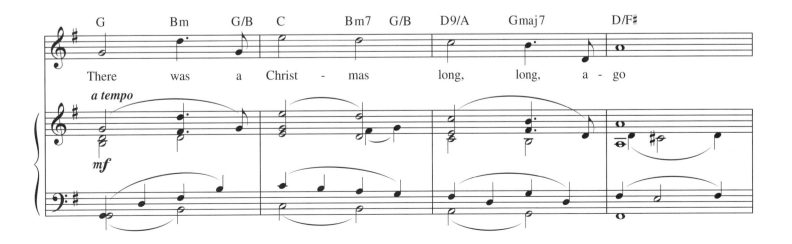

There was a Christ - mas long, long, a - go

a tempo

mf

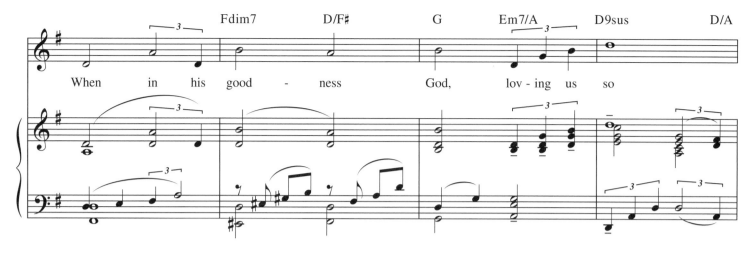

When in his good - ness God, lov - ing us so

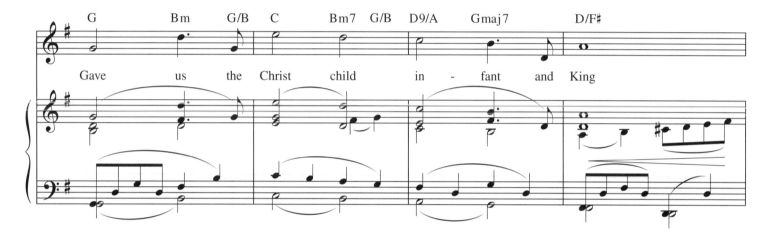

Gave us the Christ child in - fant and King

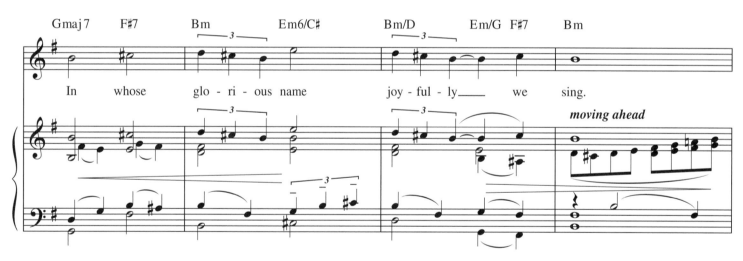

In whose glo - ri - ous name joy - ful - ly____ we sing.

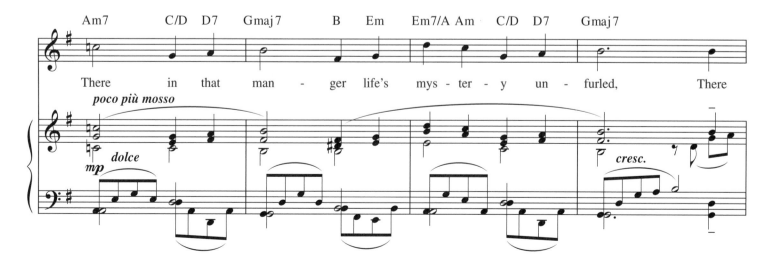

There in that man - ger life's mys - ter - y un - furled, There

BALLAD OF THE WAR WAGON

from the 1967 Motion Picture THE WAR WAGON

Words and Music by DIMITRI TIOMKIN
and NED WASHINGTON

Look at those hors - es. What are they drag - gin'? Heav - i - ly guard - ed, what is that wag - on? War ___ wag - on what does it hold? ___ War ___ wag - on, load - ed with gold. ___

Most men are fight-in' for a wag-on full of gold, ___

Scratch-in' and bit-in' for a wag-on full of gold, ___ My

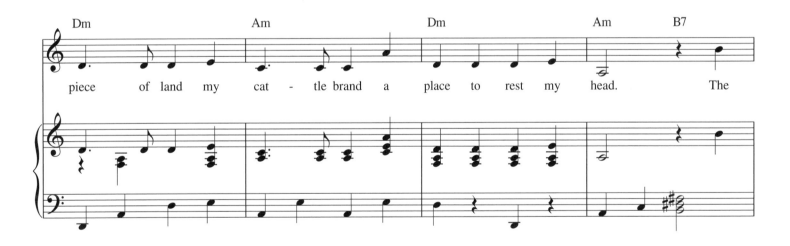

piece of land my cat - tle brand a place to rest my head. The

feel - ing of a wom - an's love are all you real - ly need for liv - in.'

Three years in pris-on made me dream a lot of dreams, _

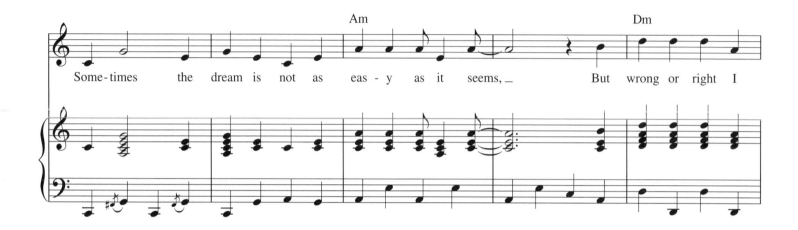

Some-times the dream is not as eas-y as it seems, _ But wrong or right I

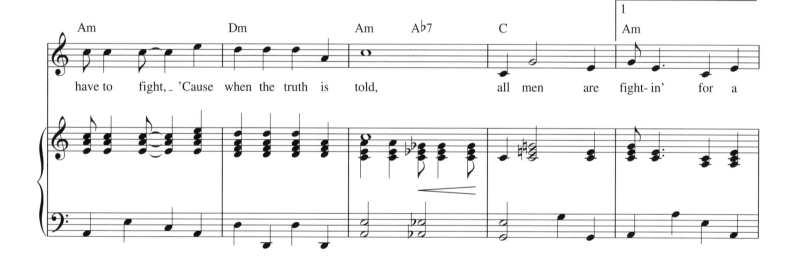

have to fight, _ 'Cause when the truth is told, all men are fight-in' for a

wag - on full of gold. Look at the hors - es. What are they drag - gin'?

Heav - i - ly guard - ed what is that wag - on?

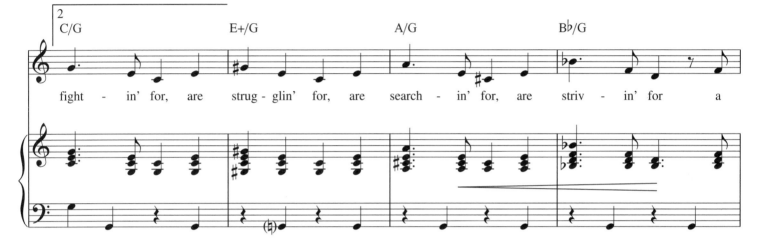

fight - in' for, are strug - glin' for, are search - in' for, are striv - in' for a

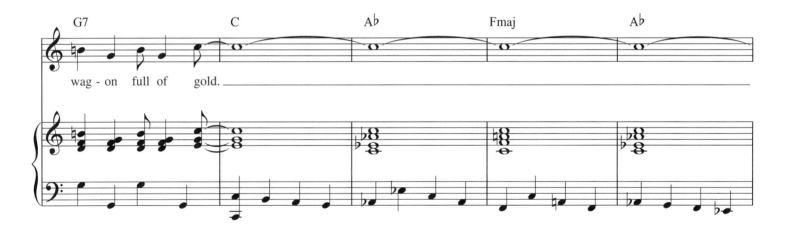

wag - on full of gold. _____

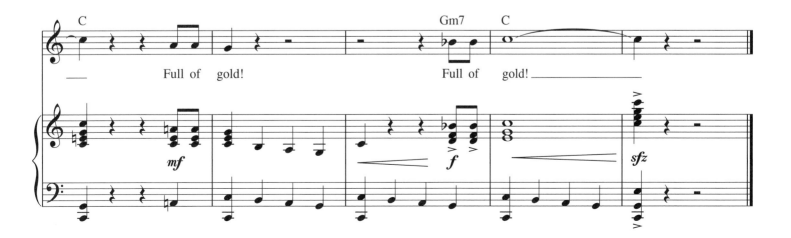

Full of gold! Full of gold! _____

THE FALL OF LOVE
from the 1964 Motion Picture THE FALL OF THE ROMAN EMPIRE

Words by NED WASHINGTON
Music by DIMITRI TIOMKIN

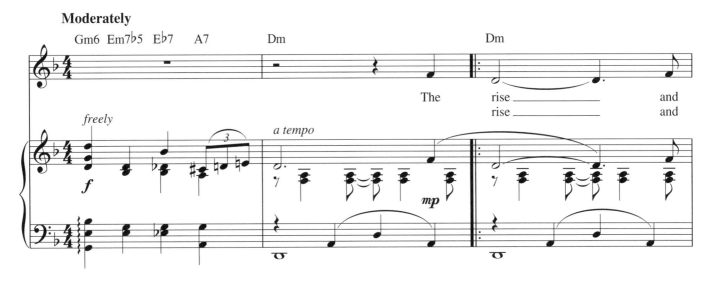

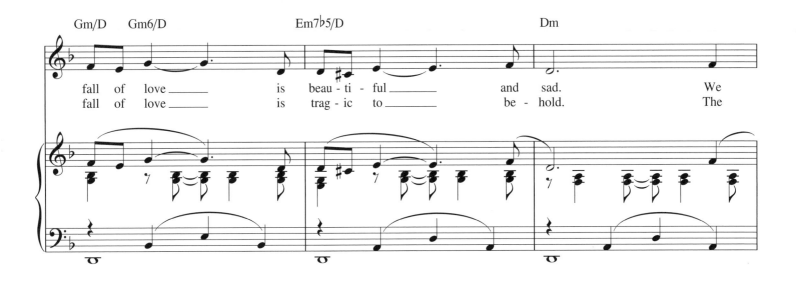

THE FALL OF LOVE
from the 1964 Motion Picture THE FALL OF THE ROMAN EMPIRE

Words by NED WASHINGTON
Music by DIMITRI TIOMKIN

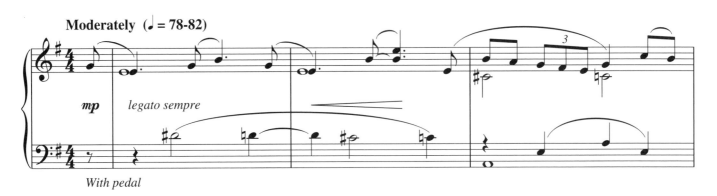

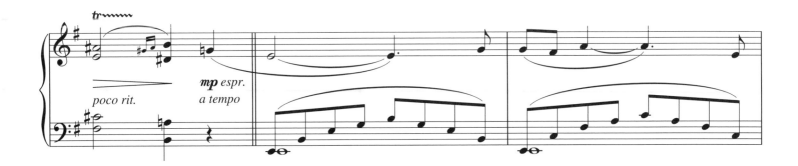

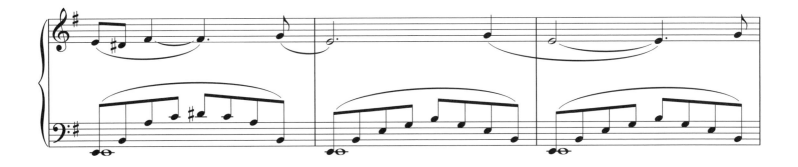

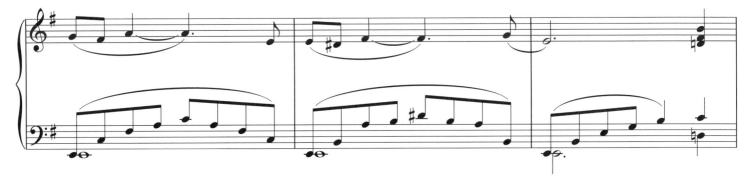

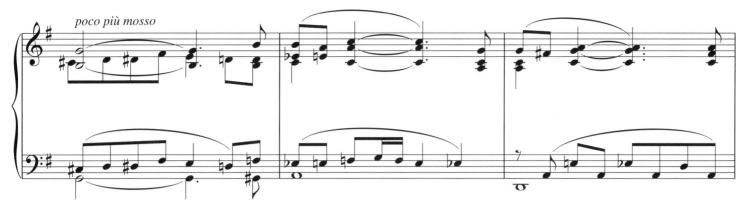

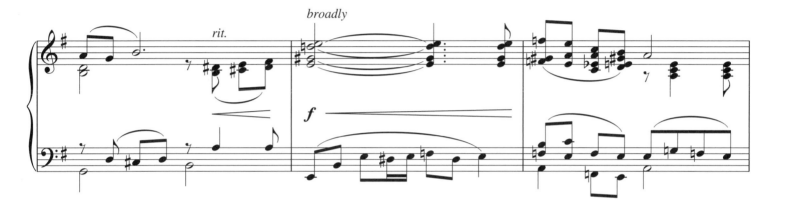

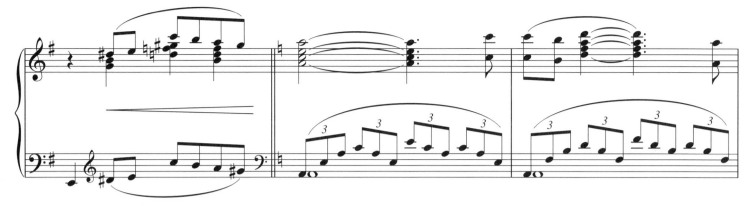

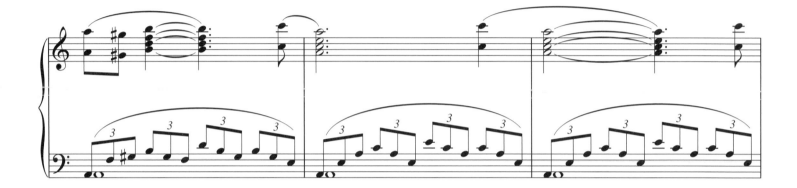

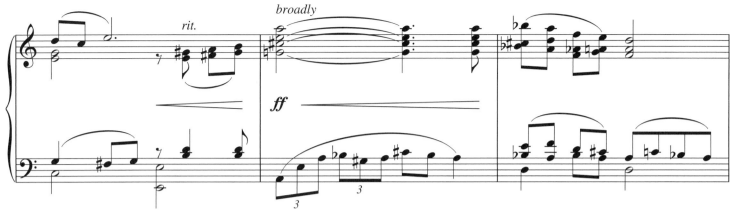

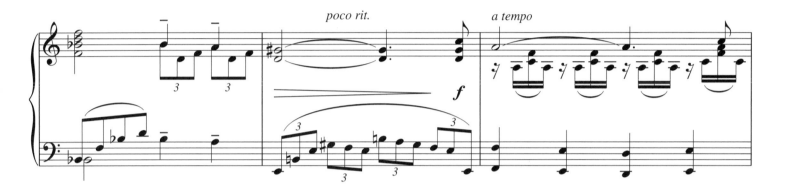

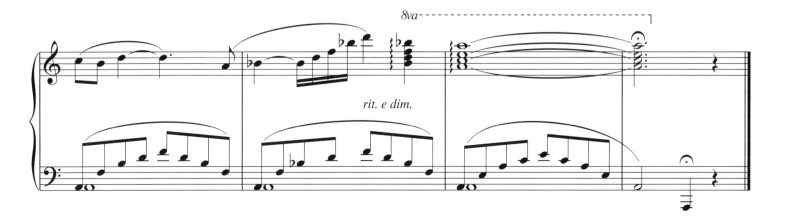

55 DAYS AT PEKING

from the 1963 Motion Picture 55 DAYS AT PEKING

Words by PAUL FRANCIS WEBSTER
Music by DIMITRI TIOMKIN

like an il-lus-tra-tion in the Sun-day mag-a-zines, you could
lev-en for-eign na-tions stood u-nit-ed, side by side, and they

To Coda

see the stars and stripes of the U-nit-ed States Ma-rines. Then
fought ten thou-sand Box-ers with a cour-age born of pride. The

came the sound of bu-gles, the roll-ing drums of doom, and the

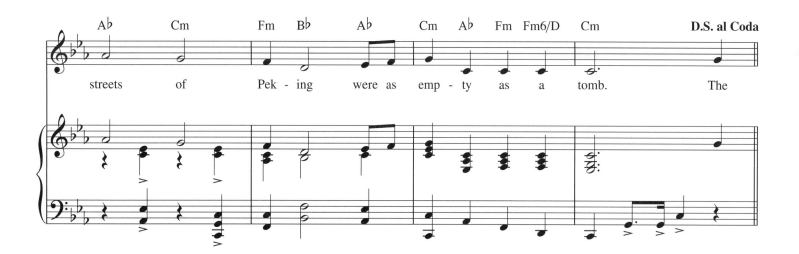

D.S. al Coda

streets of Pek-ing were as emp-ty as a tomb. The

CODA

drums have long a - go been muf - fled, the bu - gles have a rust-y ring, but down the a - ges you can hear them ech - o - ing. Fif-ty - five days at Pe - king, fif-ty - five, fif-ty - five, fif-ty - five, Fif - ty - five days at Pe - king!

FOLLOW THE RIVER

From the 1957 Picture NIGHT PASSAGE

Words and Music by NED WASHINGTON
and DIMITRI TIOMKIN

GIANT
(This Then Is Texas)
from the 1956 Motion Picture GIANT

Music by DIMITRI TIOMKIN
Words by PAUL FRANCIS WEBSTER

Rousing March tempo (♩=140)

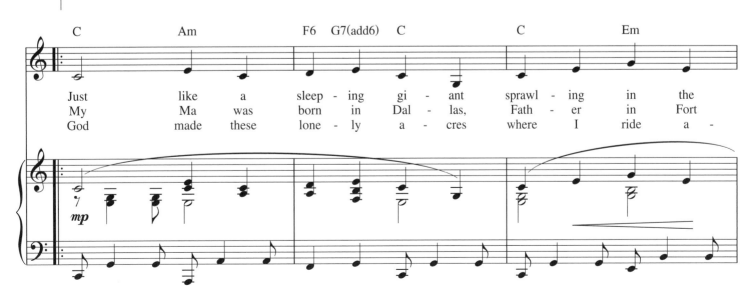

Aus - tin, and Hous - ton, and Al - a - mo, El Pas - o, Crys-tal Cit - y, Wa - co.

Just like a sleep - ing gi - ant sprawl - ing in the
My Ma was born in Dal - las, Fath - er in Fort
God made these lone - ly a - cres where I ride a -

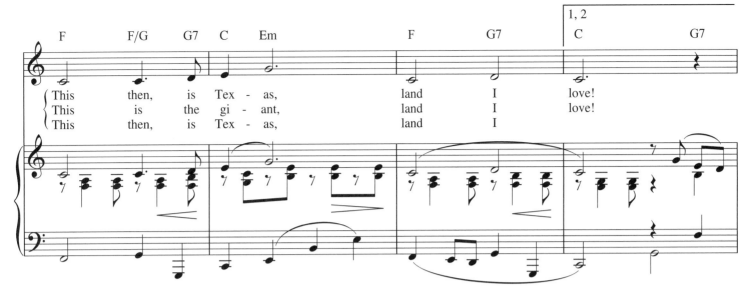

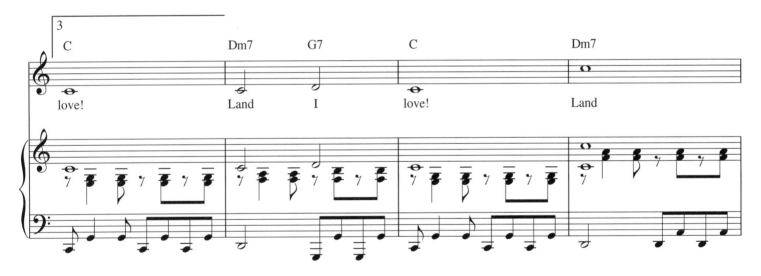

FRIENDLY PERSUASION
(Thee I Love)
from the 1956 Motion Picture FRIENDLY PERSUASION

Words by PAUL FRANCIS WEBSTER
Music by DIMITRI TIOMKIN

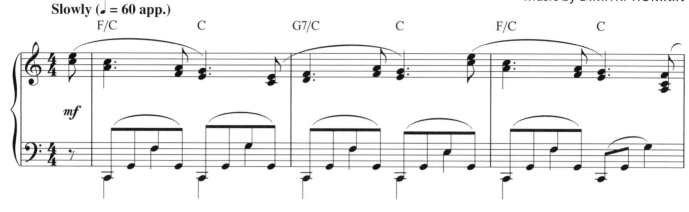

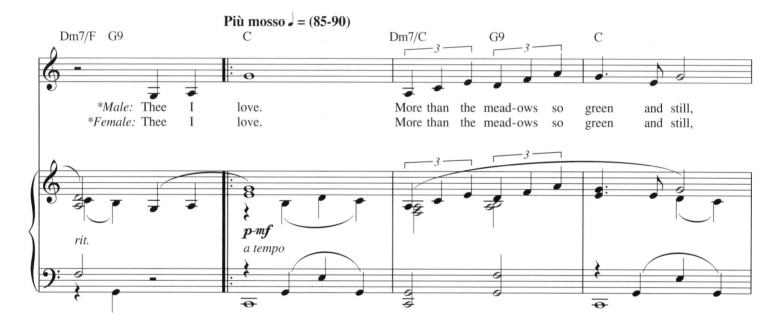

*Male: Thee I love. More than the mead-ows so green and still,
*Female: Thee I love. More than the mead-ows so green and still,

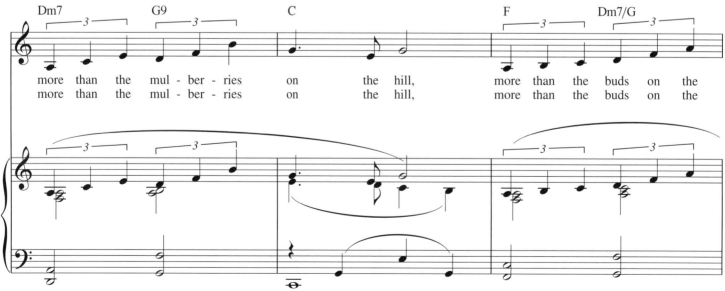

more than the mul-ber-ries on the hill, more than the buds on the
more than the mul-ber-ries on the hill, more than the buds on the

*Not a duet. Choose the appropriate lyric.

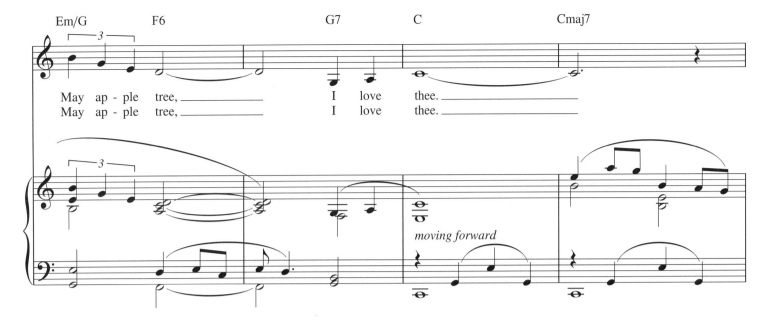

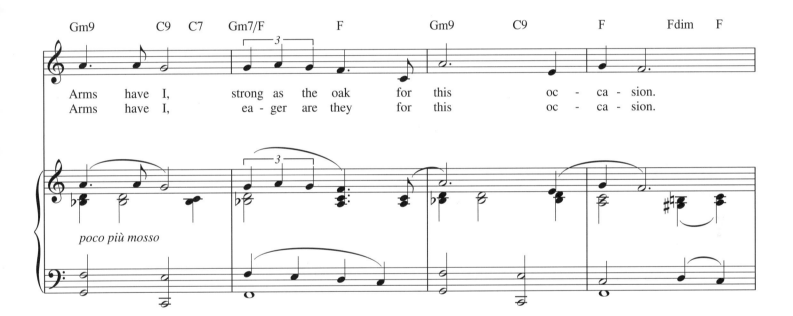

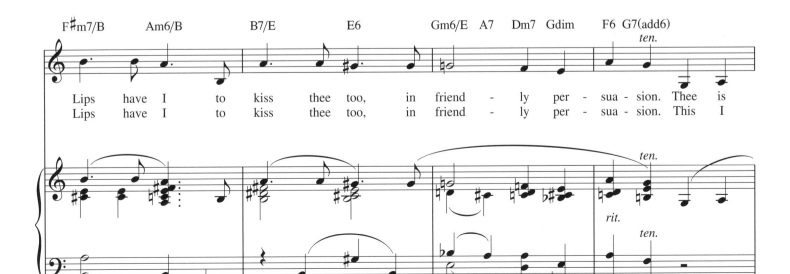

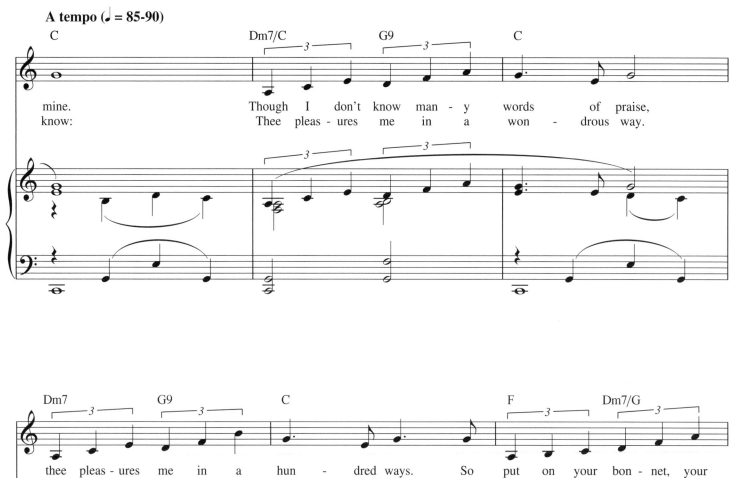

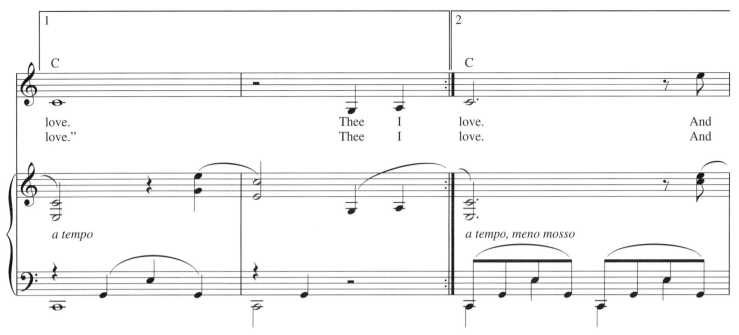

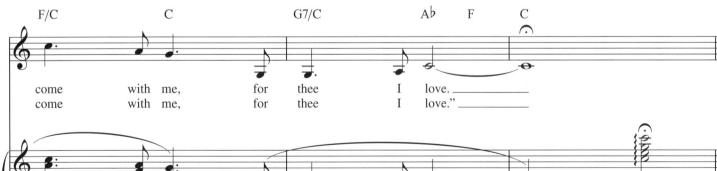

THE GREEN LEAVES OF SUMMER

from the 1960 Motion Picture THE ALAMO

Words by PAUL FRANCIS WEBSTER
Music by DIMITRI TIOMKIN

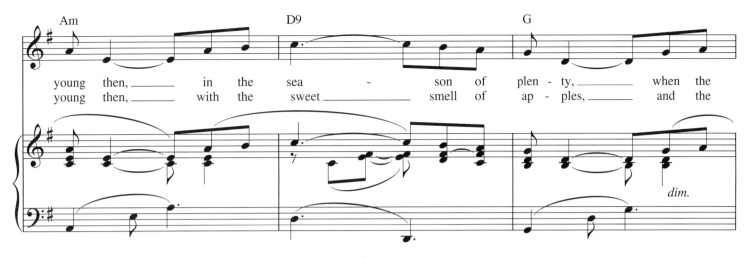

young then, _____ in the sea - son of plen - ty, _____ when the
young then, _____ with the sweet _____ smell of ap - ples, _____ and the

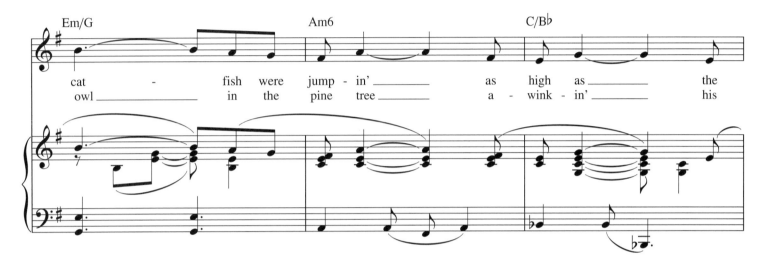

cat - fish were jump - in' _____ as high as _____ the
owl _____ in the pine tree _____ a - wink - in' _____ his

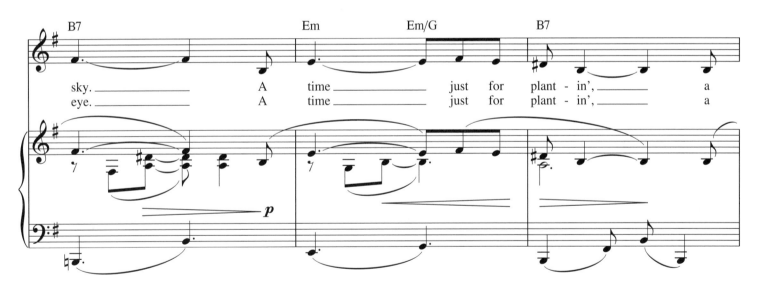

sky. _____ A time _____ just for plant - in', _____ a
eye. _____ A time _____ just for plant - in', _____ a

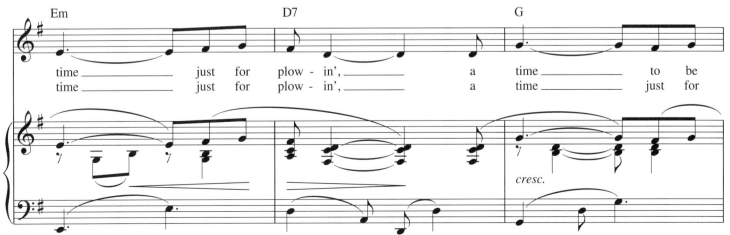

time _____ just for plow - in', _____ a time _____ to be
time _____ just for plow - in', _____ a time _____ just for

court - in' _____ a girl _____ of your own. _____ 'Twas so
liv - in', _____ a place _____ for to die. _____ 'Twas so

good _____ to be young then, _____ to be close _____ to the
good _____ to be young then, _____ to be close _____ to the

earth, _____ and to stand _____ by your wife at _____ the
earth. _____ Now the green _____ leaves of sum - mer _____ are

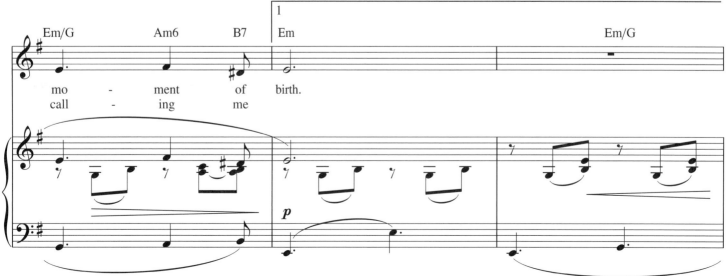

mo - ment of birth.
call - ing me

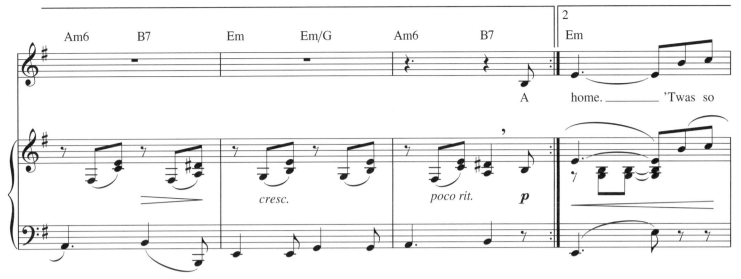

A home. _____ 'Twas so

good _____ to be young then, ____ to be close _____ to the earth. _____ Now the

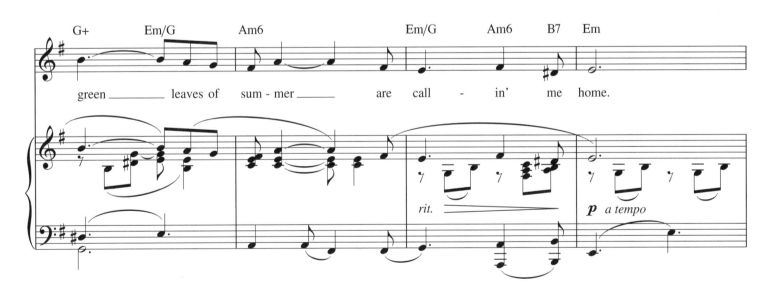

green _____ leaves of sum - mer _____ are call - in' me home.

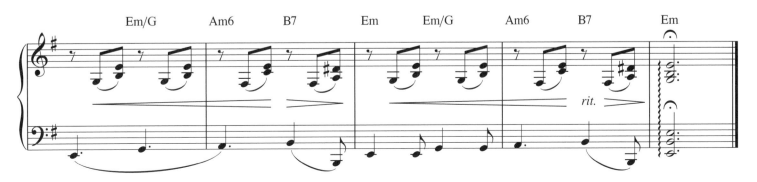

GUNFIGHT AT THE O.K. CORRAL

from the 1957 Motion Picture GUNFIGHT AT THE O.K. CORRAL

Words by NED WASHINGTON
Music by DIMITRI TIOMKIN

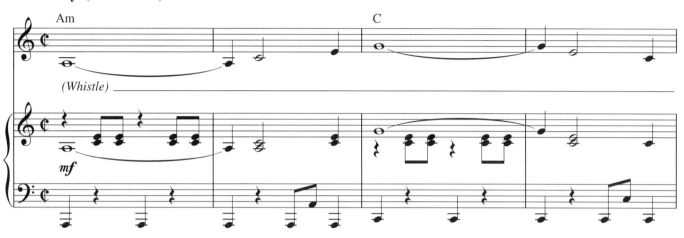

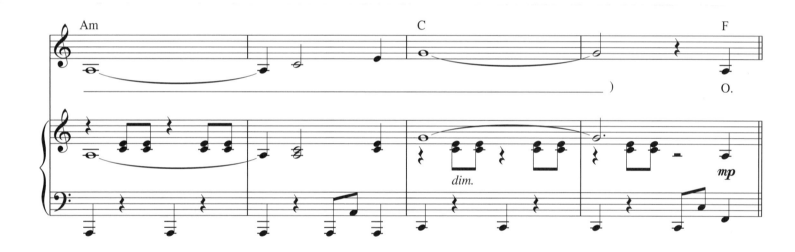

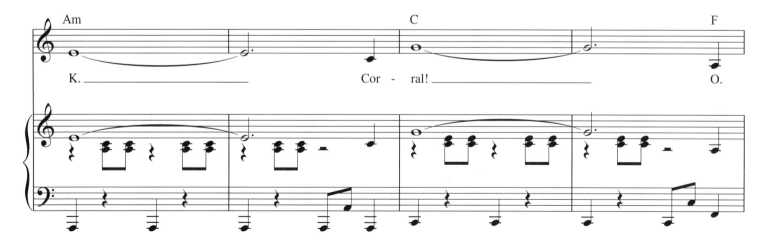

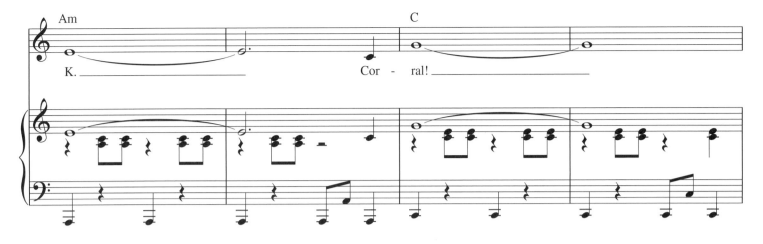

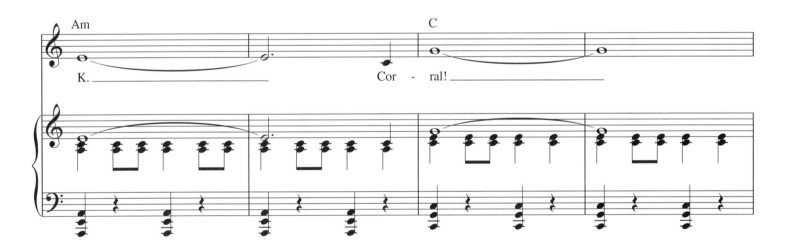

take the chance of los - ing you for - ev - er?

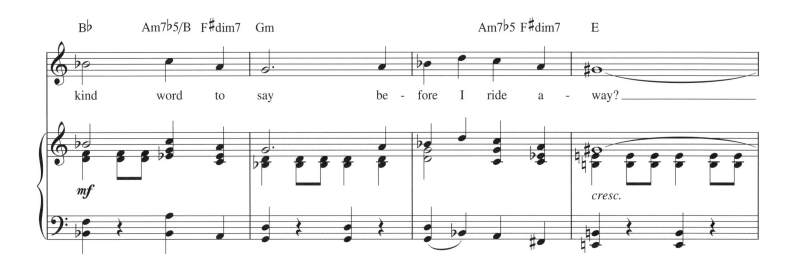

Du - ty calls, _____ my back's a - gainst the wall. _____ Have you no

kind word to say be - fore I ride a - way? _____

_____ a - way? _____ Your love, _____

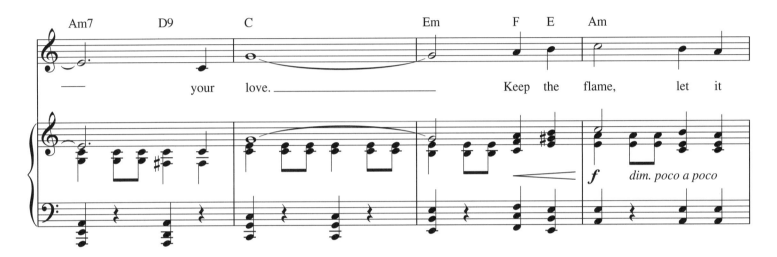

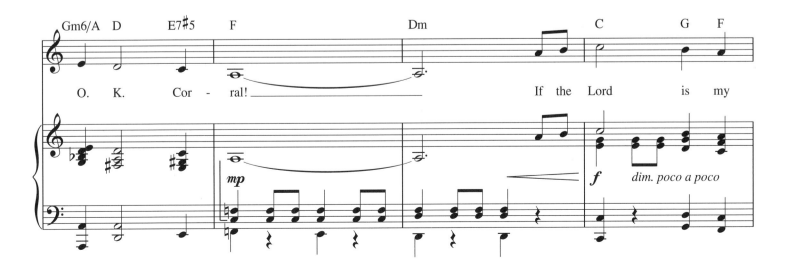

friend, we'll meet at the end of the

gun - fight at O. K. Cor - ral! _____

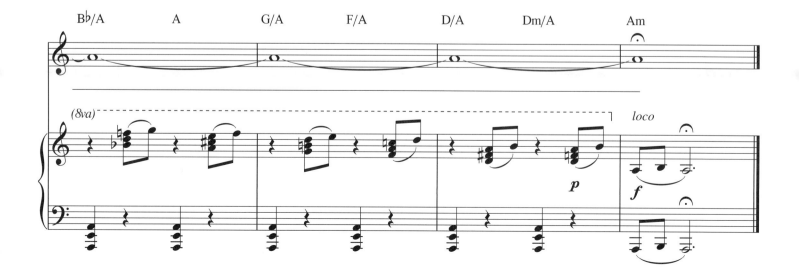

THE GUNS OF NAVARONE

from the 1961 Motion Picture THE GUNS OF NAVARONE

Words and Music by DIMITRI TIOMKIN
and PAUL WEBSTER
Arranged by Paul Henning

Lyrics:

Is - lands of Greece are green and beau - ti - ful, green and beau - ti - ful where the ol - ive trees

grow._____ In the fields be - low._____ But

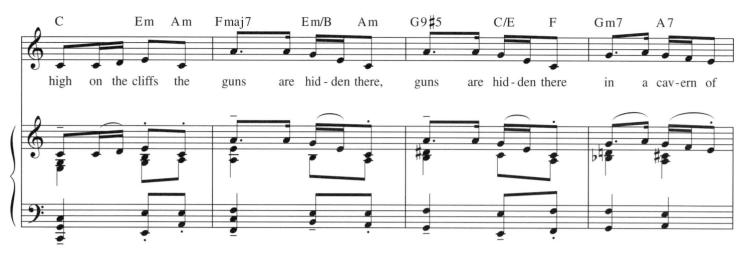

high on the cliffs the guns are hid-den there, guns are hid-den there in a cav-ern of

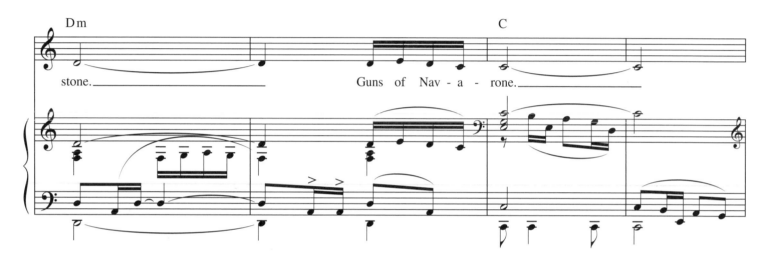

stone. _____ Guns of Nav-a-rone. _____

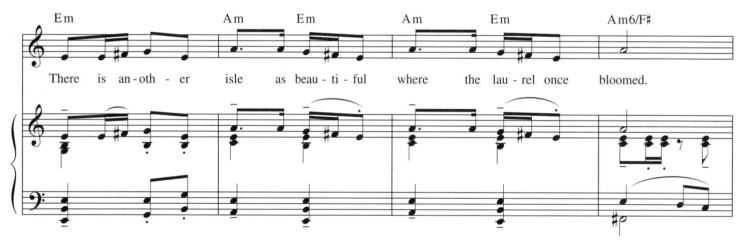

There is an-oth-er isle as beau-ti-ful where the lau-rel once bloomed.

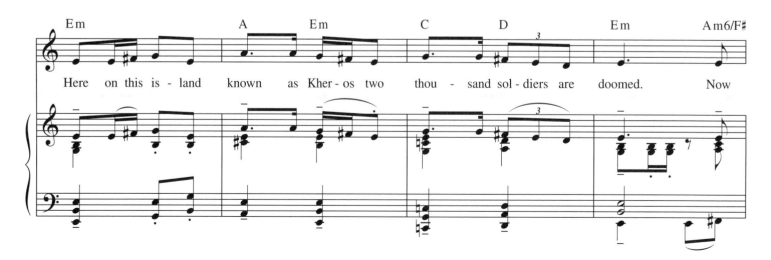

Here on this is-land known as Kher-os two thou-sand sol-diers are doomed. Now

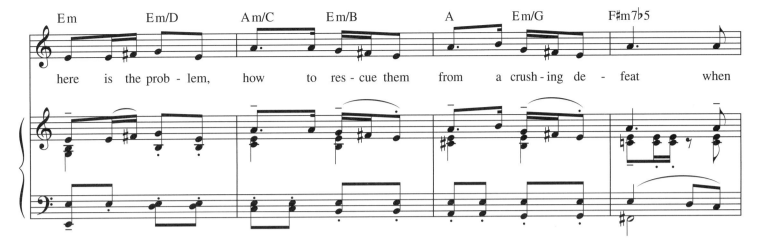

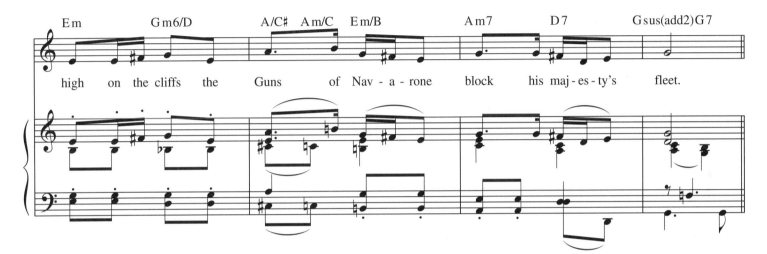

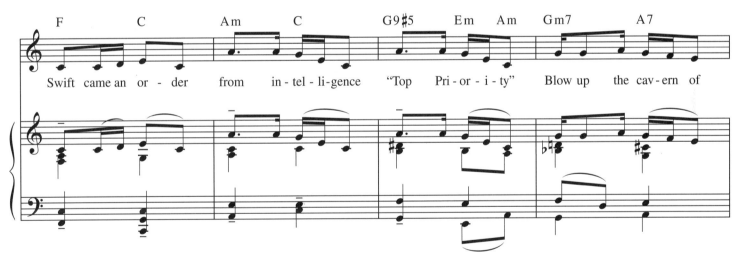

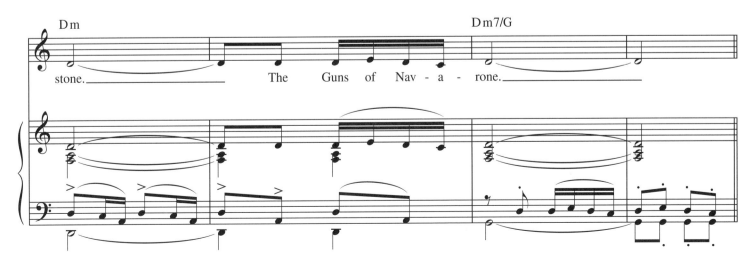

54

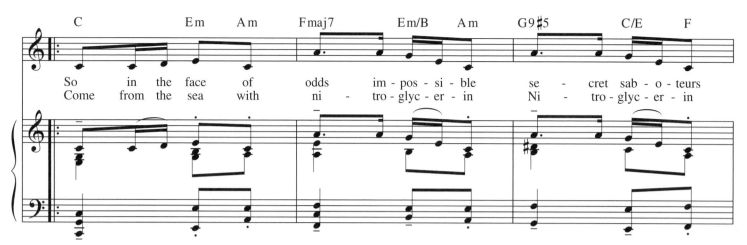

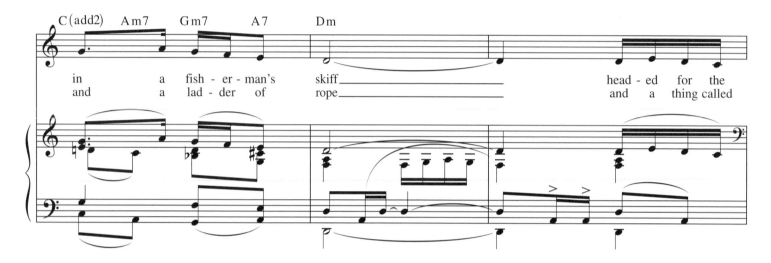

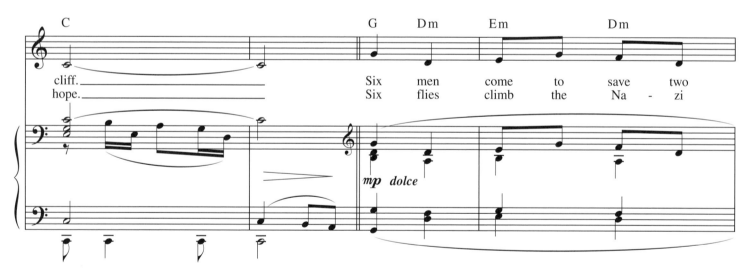

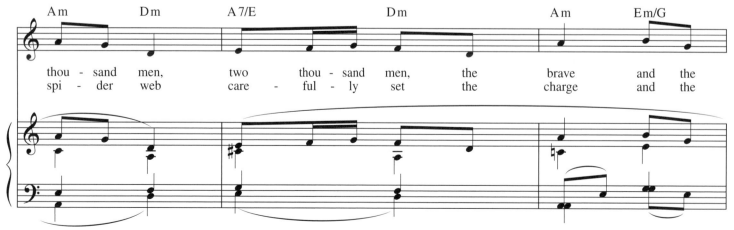

GUNSLINGER

Theme from the 1961 Television Series GUNSLINGER

Words by NED WASHINGTON
Music by DIMITRI TIOMKIN

March (♩ = c. 120)

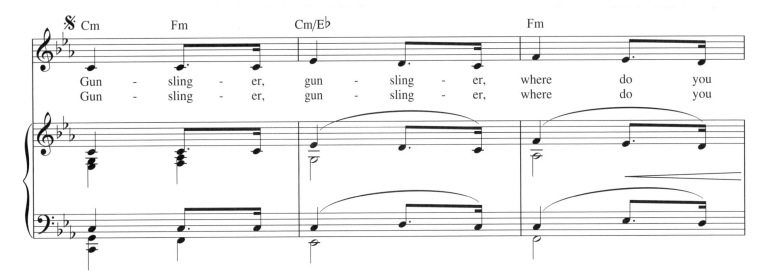

Gun - sling - er, gun - sling - er, where do you
Gun - sling - er, gun - sling - er, where do you

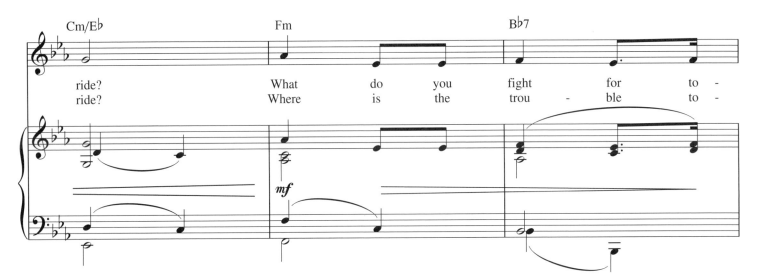

ride? What do you fight for to -
ride? Where is the trou - ble to -

HEADIN' HOME
from the 1946 Motion Picture DUEL IN THE SUN

Music by DIMITRI TIOMKIN
Words by FREDERICK HERBERT

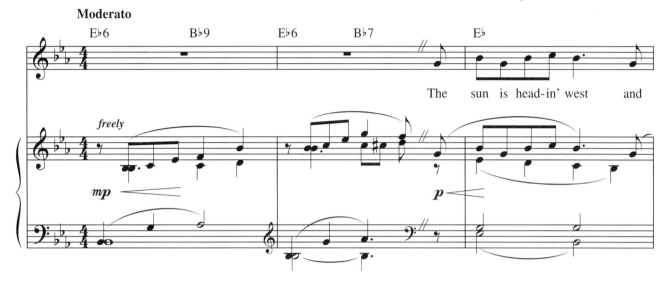

The sun is head-in' west and

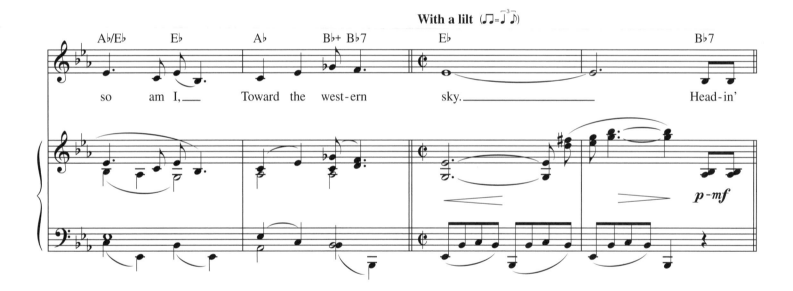

so am I, ___ Toward the west-ern sky. _____ Head-in'

Home, _____ Head-in' Home, _____ The wag-on wheels are crunch-in' on the grav-el; _____ They

THE HIGH AND THE MIGHTY

from the 1954 Motion Picture THE HIGH AND THE MIGHTY

Words by NED WASHINGTON
Music by DIMITRI TIOMKIN

HIGH NOON
(Do Not Forsake Me)
from the 1952 Motion Picture HIGH NOON

Words by NED WASHINGTON
Music by DIMITRI TIOMKIN

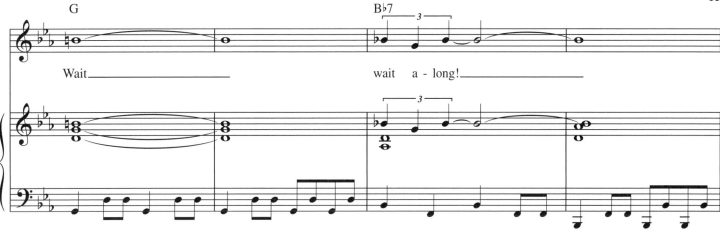

Wait_____ wait a - long!_____

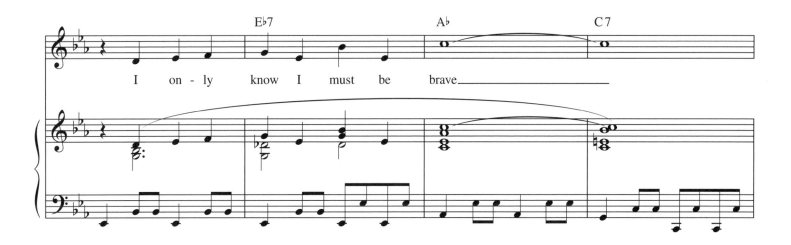

I do not know what fate a - waits me_____

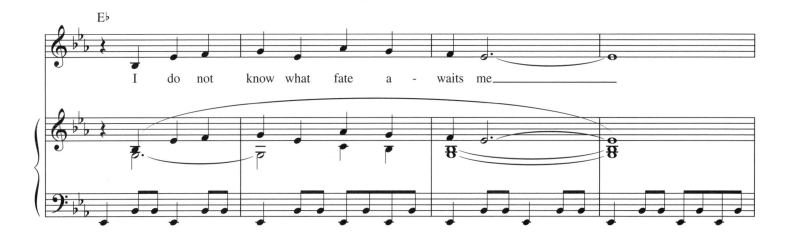

I on - ly know I must be brave_____

And I must face a man who hates me_____

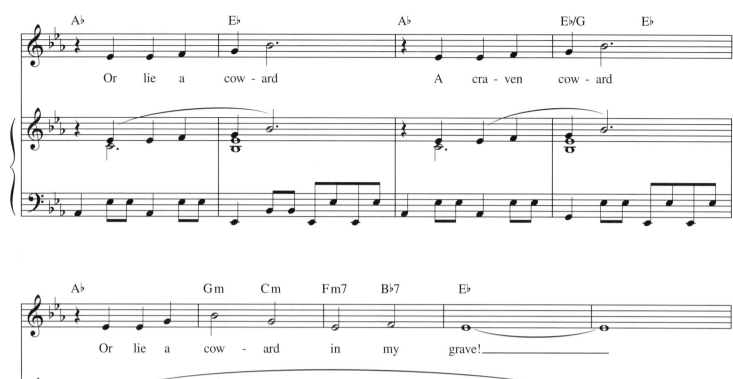

Or lie a cow - ard A cra - ven cow - ard

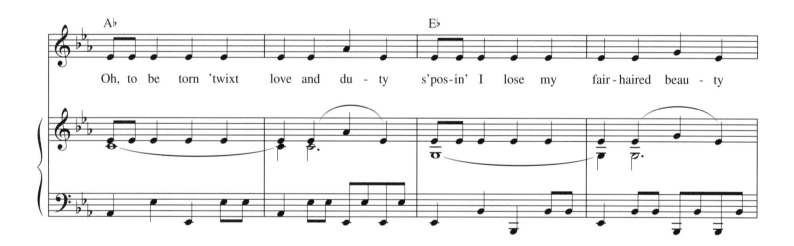

Or lie a cow - ard in my grave! _____

Oh, to be torn 'twixt love and du - ty s'pos-in' I lose my fair-haired beau - ty

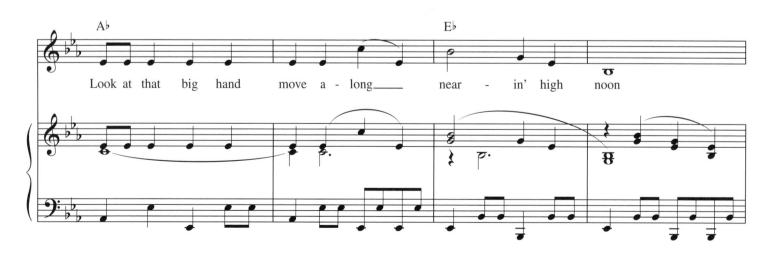

Look at that big hand move a - long ____ near - in' high noon

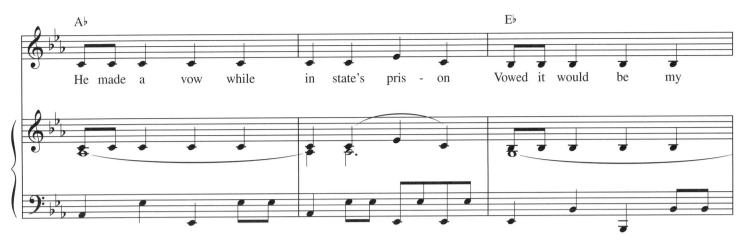

He made a vow while in state's pris - on Vowed it would be my

life or his - 'n I'm not a - fraid of death but, oh_____

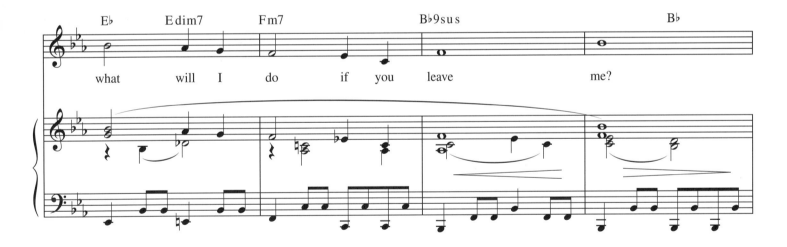

what will I do if you leave me?

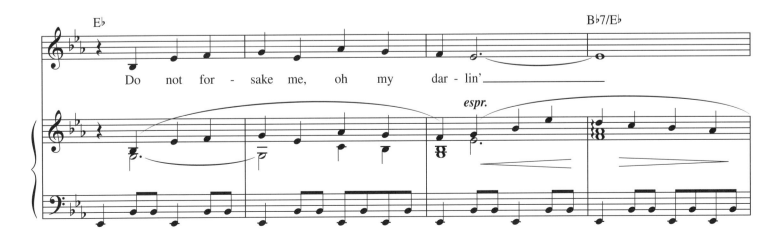

Do not for - sake me, oh my dar - lin'_____

72

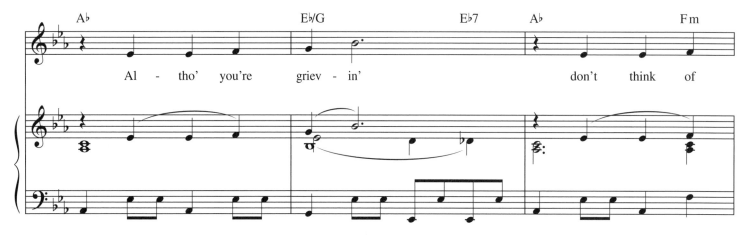

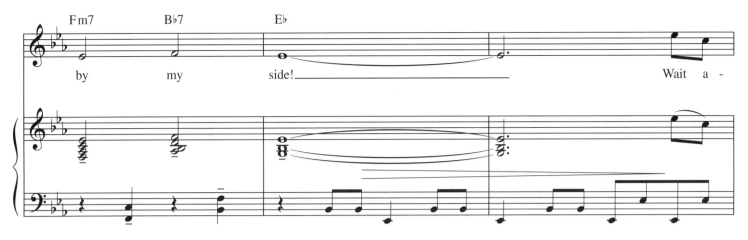

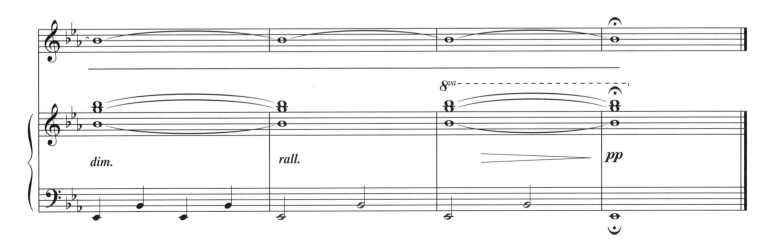

I'LL BALLYHOO YOU

from the 1932 Stage Musical THE LITTLE RACKETEER

Music by DIMITRI TIOMKIN
Words by EDWARD ELISCU

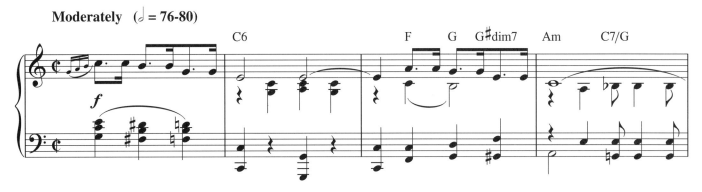

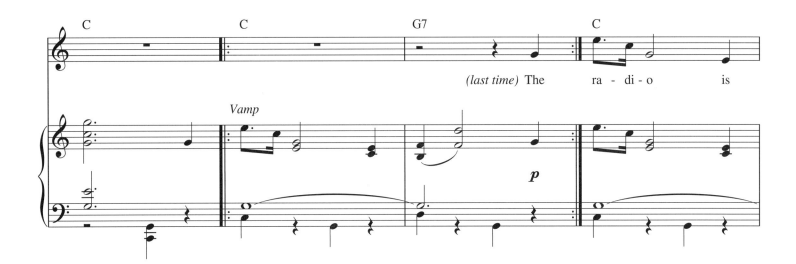

(last time) The ra - di - o is

great ad - ver - tis - ing _____ for tell - ing and

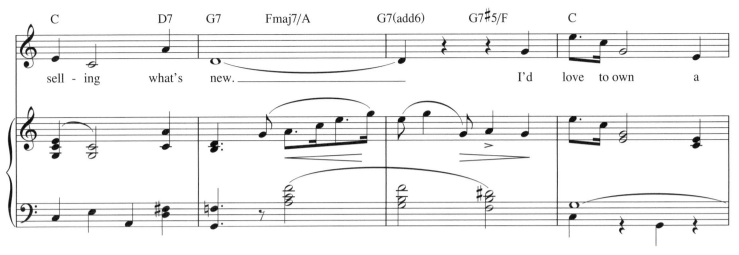

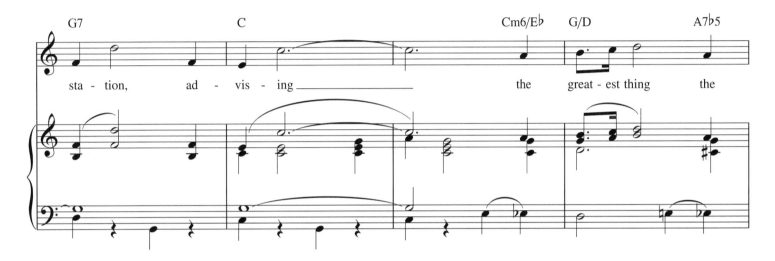

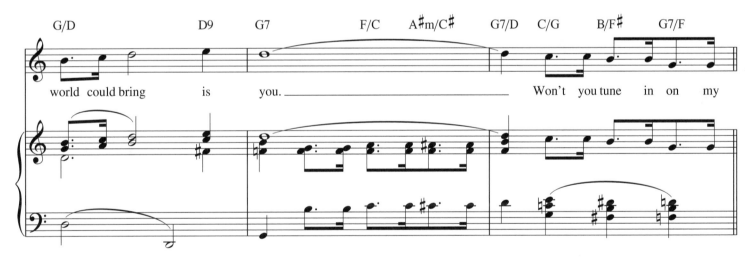

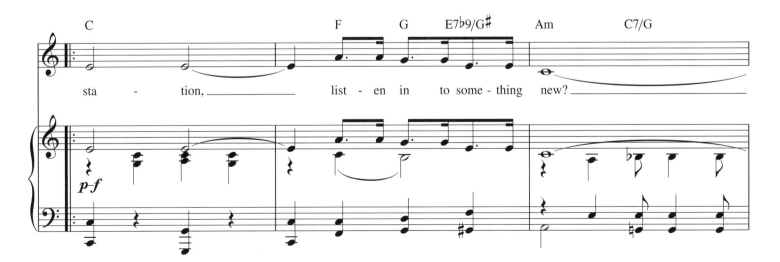

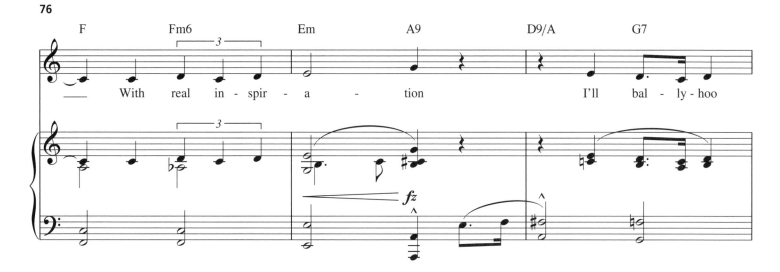

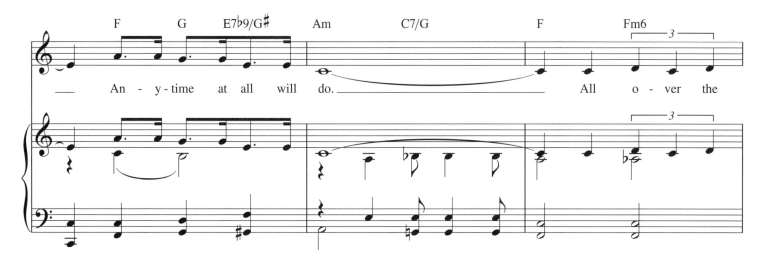

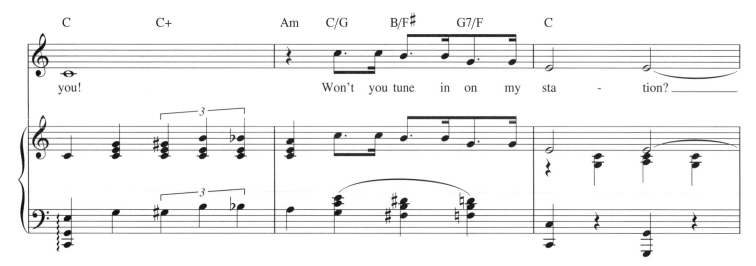

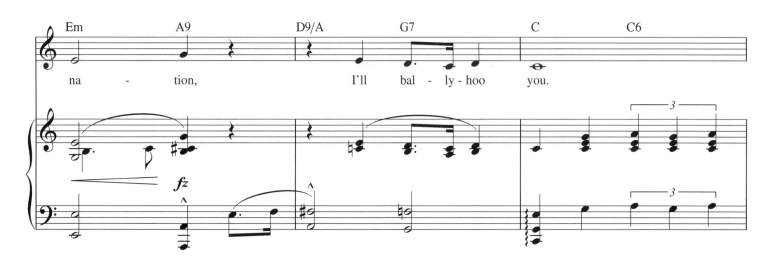

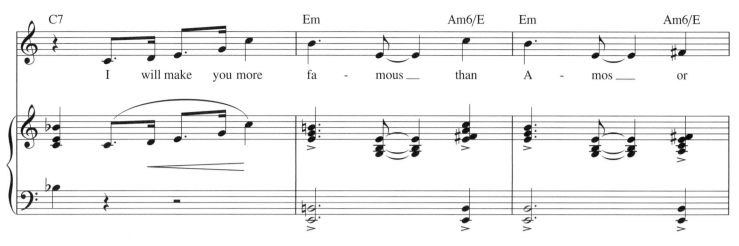

I will make you more fa - mous than A - mos or

And - y were an - y - where. Each wave length, _ a

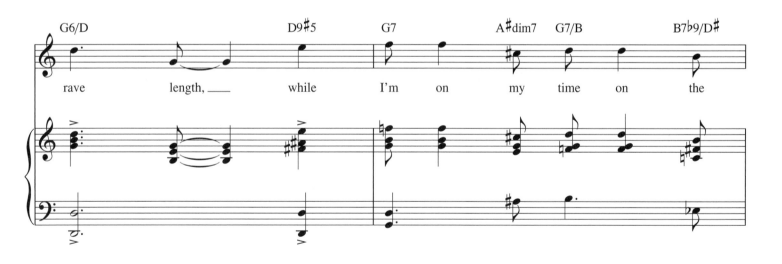

rave length, _____ while I'm on my time on the

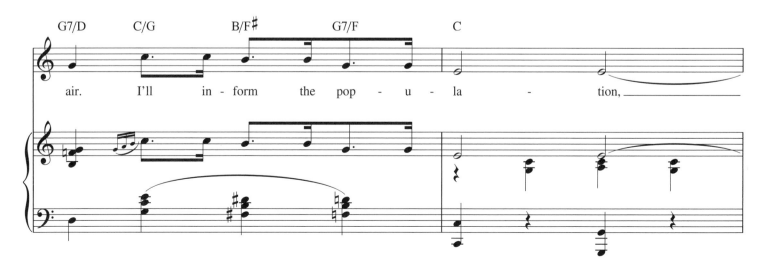

air. I'll in - form the pop - u - la - tion, _____

and they'll want to meet you, too, _____ when o - ver my

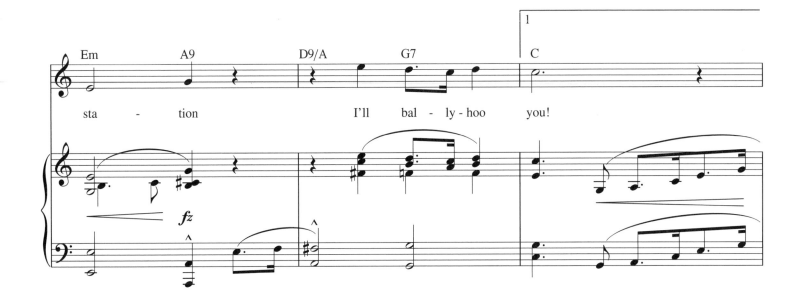

sta - tion I'll bal - ly - hoo you!

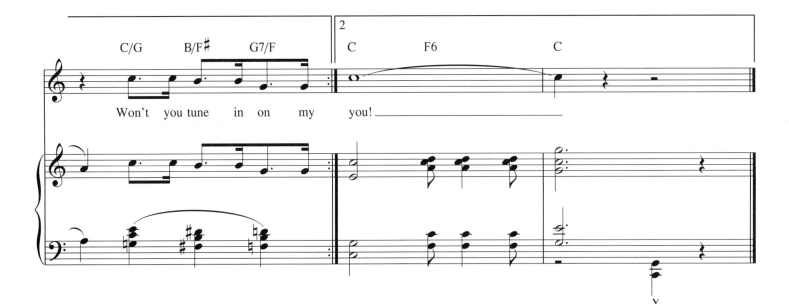

Won't you tune in on my you! _____

IT'S A WONDERFUL LIFE

from the 1946 Motion Picture IT'S A WONDERFUL LIFE

Words by FREDERICK HERBERT
Music by DIMITRI TIOMKIN

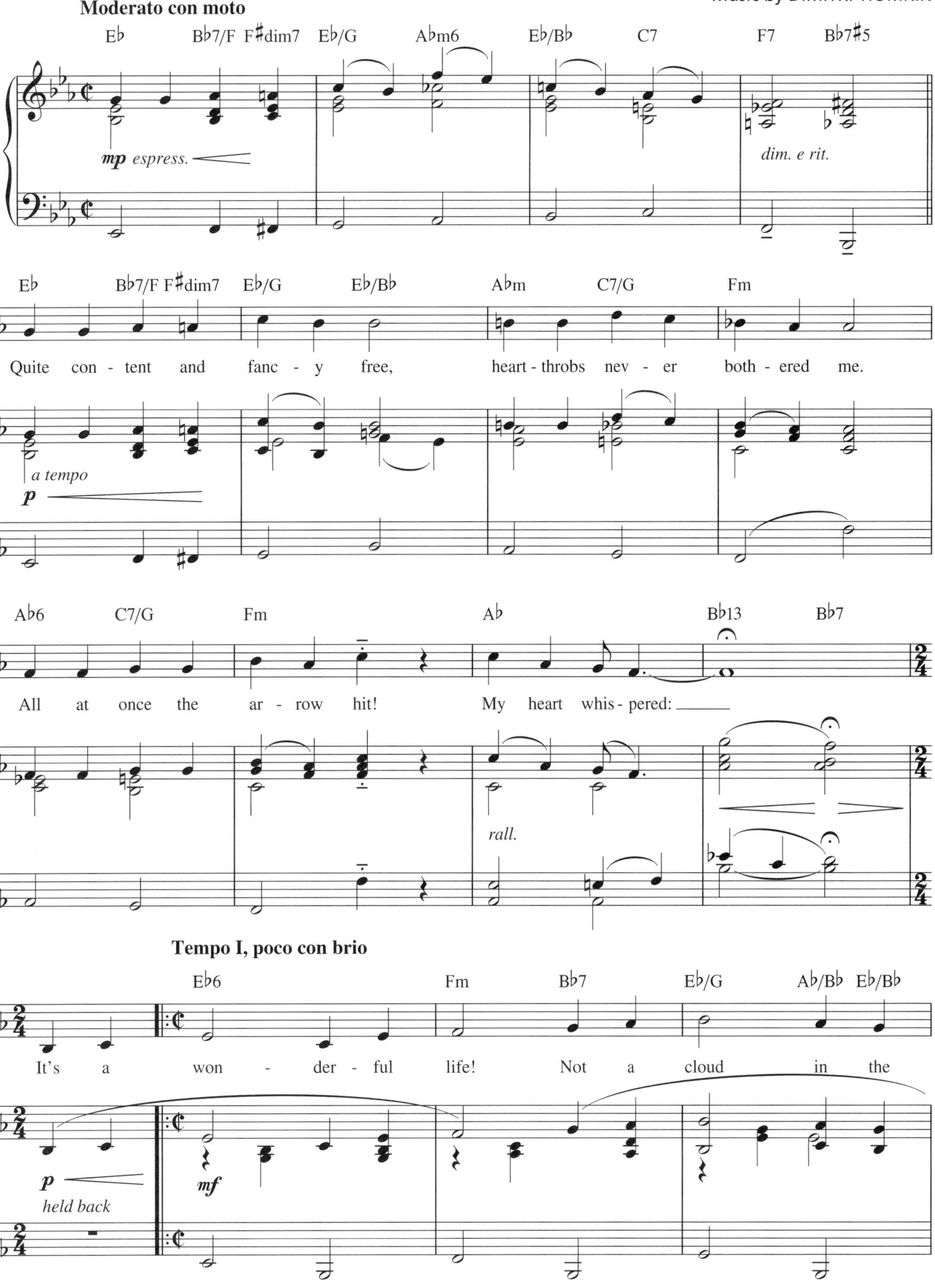

Moderato con moto
E♭ B♭7/F F♯dim7 E♭/G A♭m6 E♭/B♭ C7 F7 B♭7♯5
mp espress.
dim. e rit.
E♭ B♭7/F F♯dim7 E♭/G E♭/B♭ A♭m C7/G Fm
Quite con - tent and fanc - y free, heart - throbs nev - er both - ered me.
a tempo
p
A♭6 C7/G Fm A♭ B♭13 B♭7
All at once the ar - row hit! My heart whis - pered:
rall.
Tempo I, poco con brio
E♭6 Fm B♭7 E♭/G A♭/B♭ E♭/B♭
It's a won - der - ful life! Not a cloud in the
p
held back
mf

80

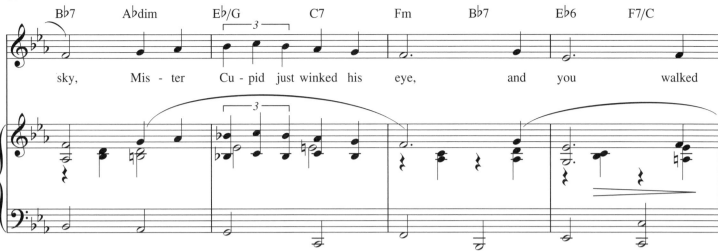

sky, Mis- ter Cu- pid just winked his eye, and you walked

by. It's a won- der- ful life! I have more than my

share, see me walk- ing a- round on air, be- cause you care. _____

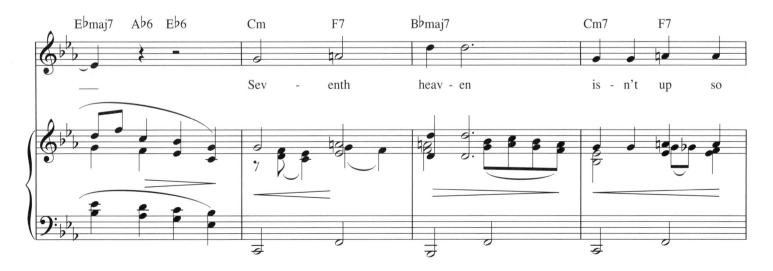

Sev - enth heav - en is - n't up so

INDIANA HOLIDAY

from the 1956 Motion Picture FRIENDLY PERSUASION

Words and Music by DIMITRI TIOMKIN
and PAUL WEBSTER

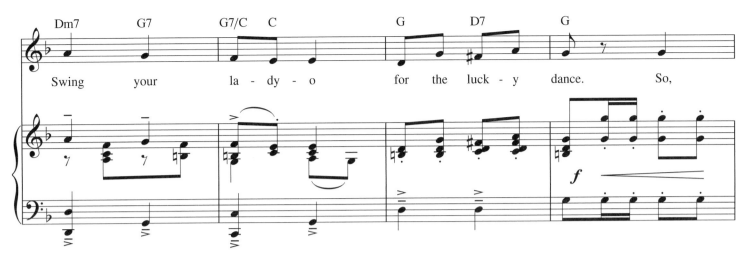

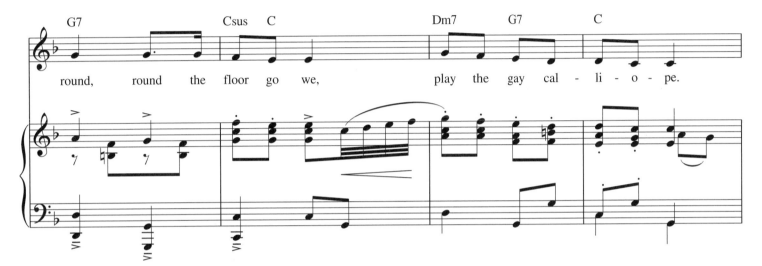

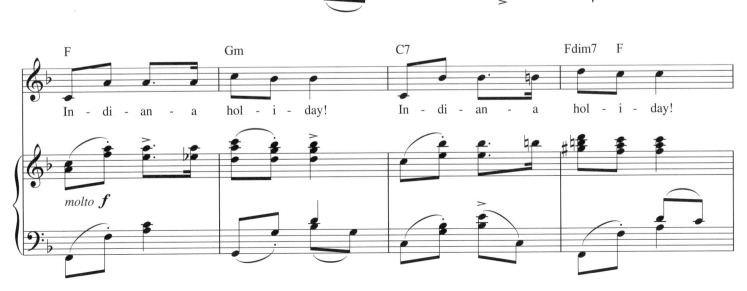

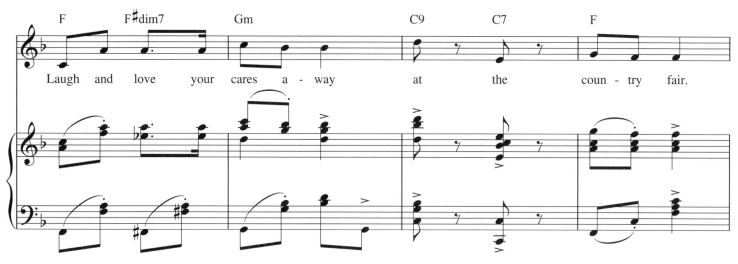

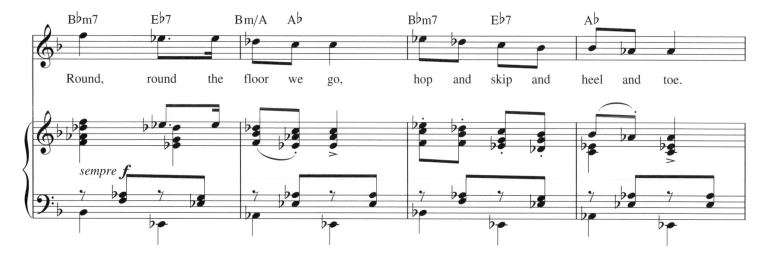

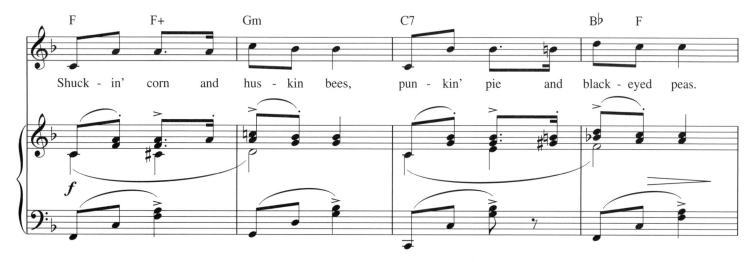

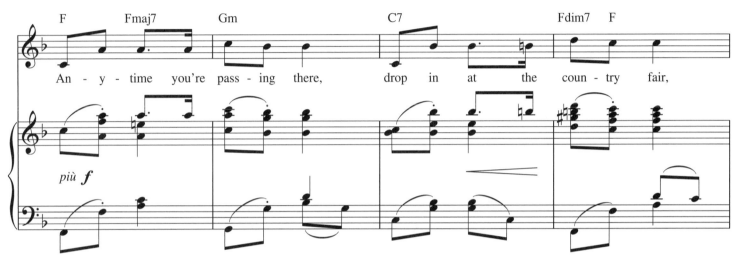

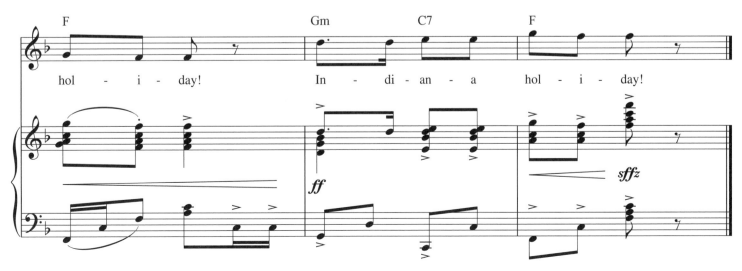

JETT RINK BALLAD
(The James Dean Theme)
from the 1956 Motion Picture GIANT

Music by DIMITRI TIOMKIN
Words by PAUL FRANCIS WEBSTER
Arranged Paul Henning

JULIE

from the 1953 Motion Picture TAKE THE HIGH GROUND

Music by DIMITRI TIOMKIN
Words by CHARLES WALCOTT

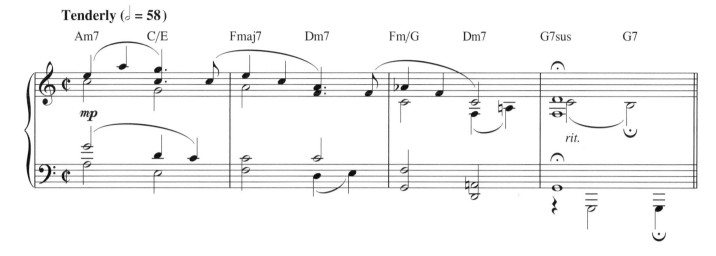

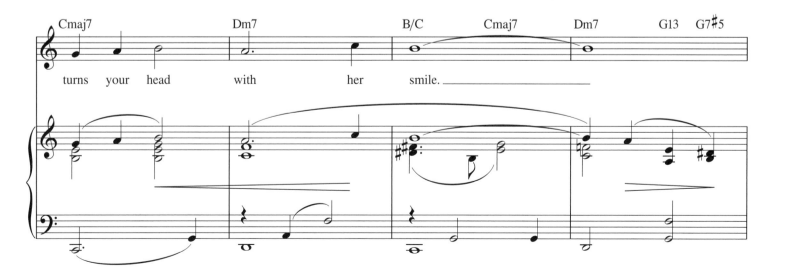

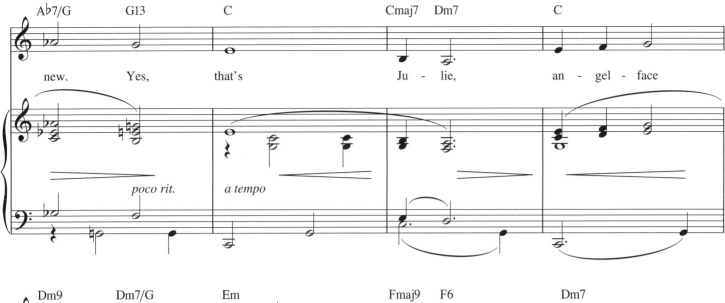

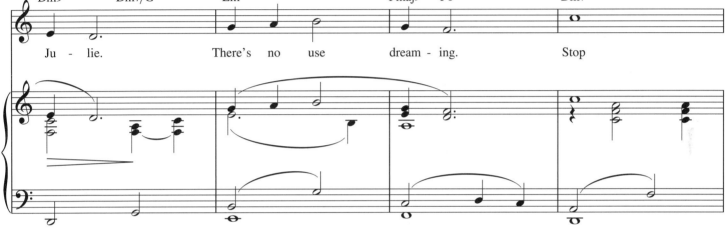

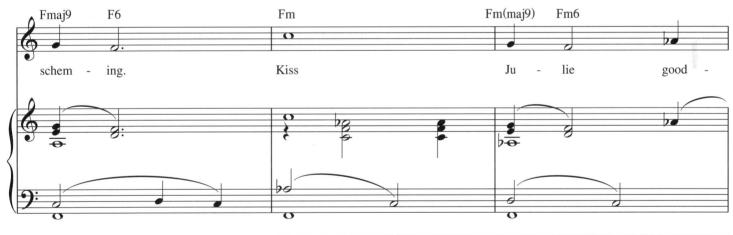

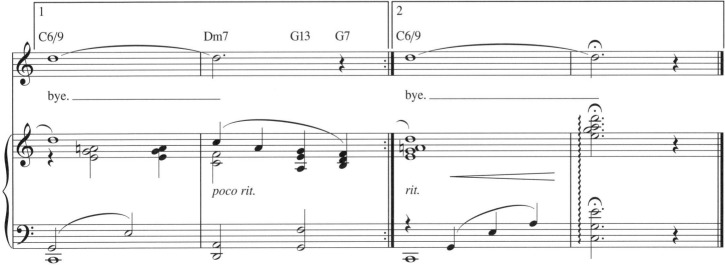

JOHN WAYNE MARCH

from the 1964 Motion Picture CIRCUS WORLD

By DIMITRI TIOMKIN

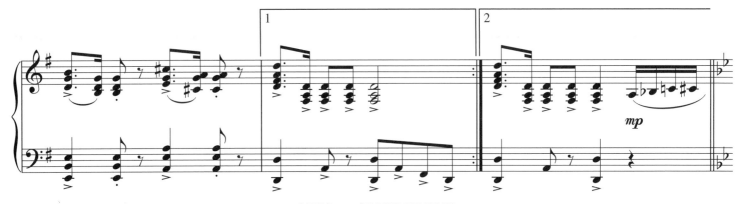

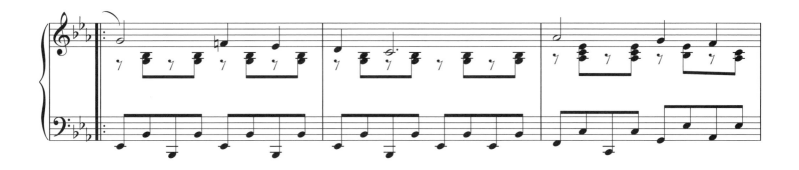

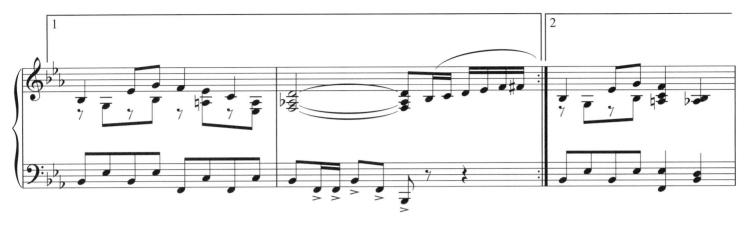

KASHMIR
from the 1957 Motion Picture SEARCH FOR PARADISE

Words by NED WASHINGTON
and LOWELL THOMAS
Music by DIMITRI TIOMKIN

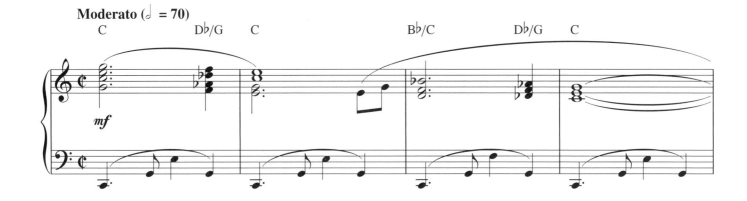

Kash - mir, Kash - mir! Life is joy, life is full of

cheer! Kash - mir, oh, Kash - mir! Cut - rate par - a - dise this time of

To Coda ⊕

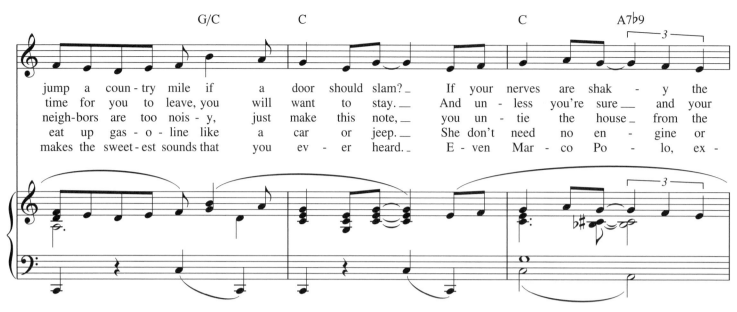

Verses 1-4: D.S.
Verse 5: D.S. al Coda

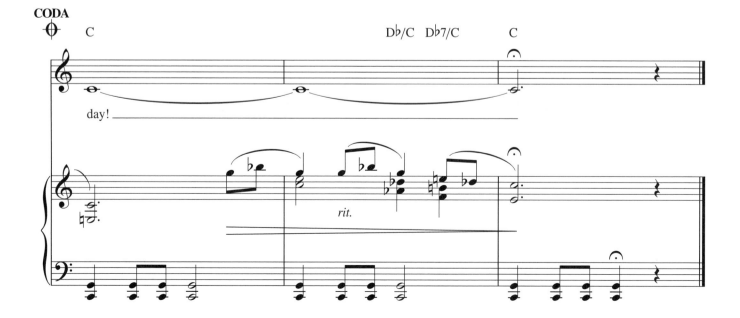

LAND OF THE PHARAOHS

from the 1955 Motion Picture LAND OF THE PHARAOHS

Music by DIMITRI TIOMKIN
Words by NED WASHINGTON
Arranged Paul Henning

LAST TRAIN FROM GUN HILL

from the 1959 Motion Picture LAST TRAIN FROM GUN HILL

Music by DIMITRI TIOMKIN
Words by PAUL FRANCIS WEBSTER
Arranged Paul Henning

LOVE LIKE OURS

from the 1950 Motion Picture THE MEN

Words by JOHNNY LEHMAN
Music by DIMITRI TIOMKIN
Arranged Paul Henning

LOST HORIZON
(Adieux)
from the 1937 Motion Picture LOST HORIZON

Words by GUS KAHN
Music by DIMITRI TIOMKIN

Lento tranquillo: dolce e legato sempre ♩ = (70-75)

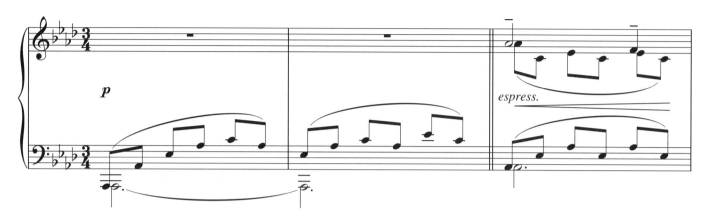

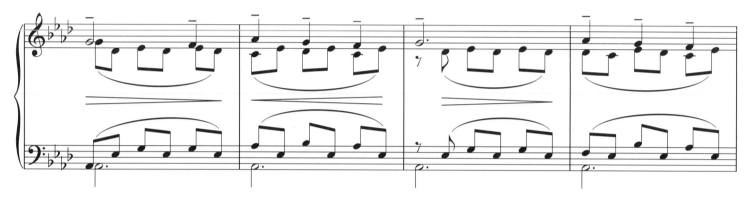

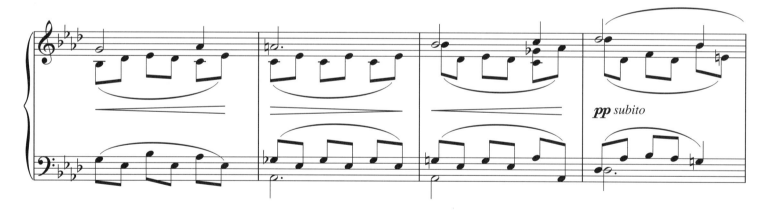

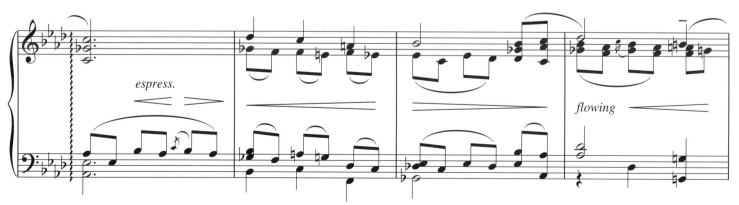

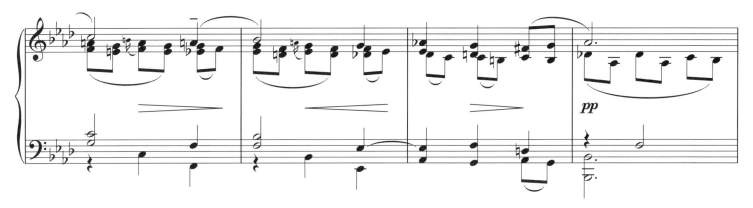

Poco meno mosso

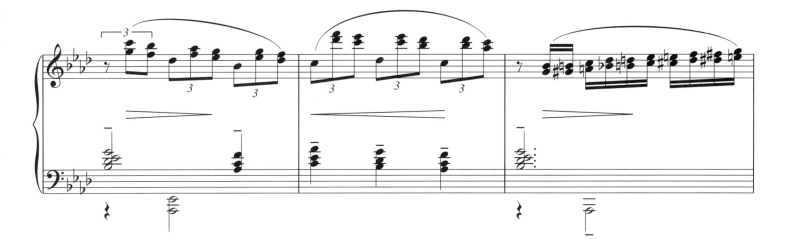

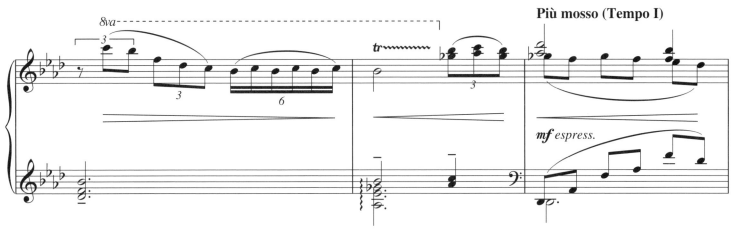

Più mosso (Tempo I)

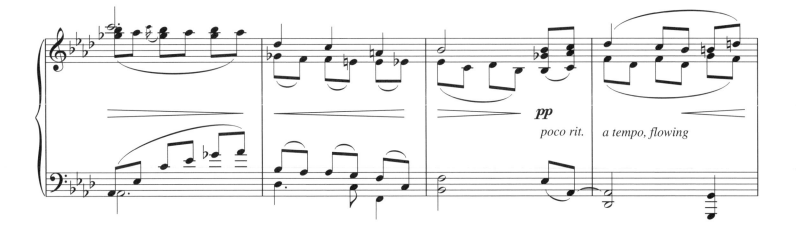

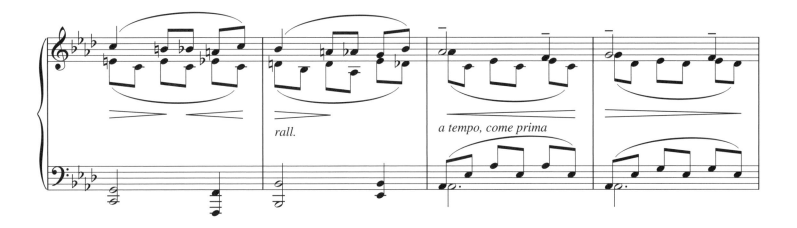

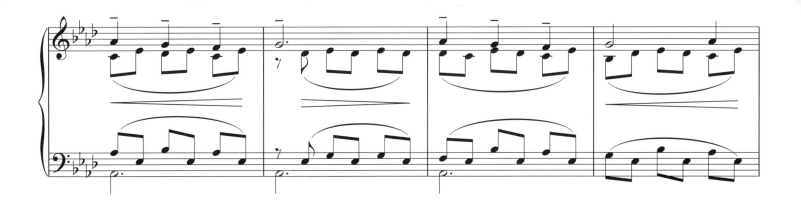

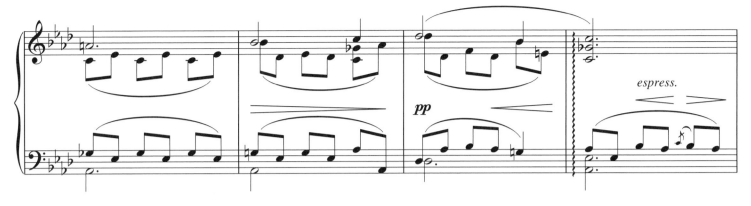

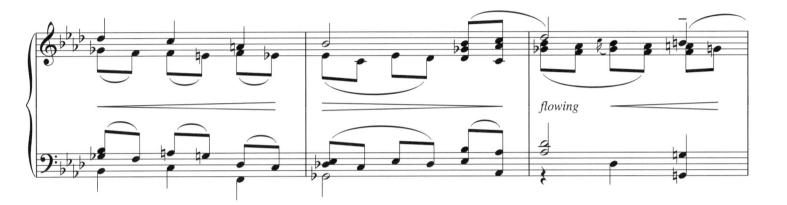

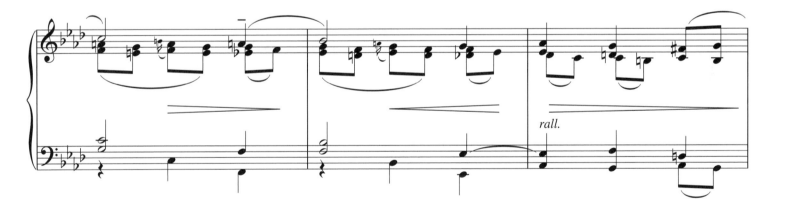

Lento molto al fine

LOVE, LOOK WHAT YOU'VE DONE TO ME

from the 1953 Motion Picture I CONFESS

Music by DIMITRI TIOMKIN
Words by NED WASHINGTON

THE NEED FOR LOVE

from the 1960 Motion Picture THE UNFORGIVEN

Words and Music by DIMITRI TIOMKIN
and NED WASHINGTON

por - tant than world - ly af - fairs._____ And to the ones who are still un - for -

giv - en,_____ love is a food and they need ev - 'ry crumb,_____ a thing that's

treas - ured_____ that can't be meas - ured_____ by an - y scale or rule of thumb.

moving ahead

Some - times_____ hearts are driv - en in - to their own lit - tle shell,

poco più mosso

MY FAVORITE MEMORY

from the 1954 Motion Picture DIAL M FOR MURDER

Lyric by JACK LAWRENCE
Music by DIMITRI TIOMKIN
Arranged Paul Henning

Moderato
freely

Yes, I love you still and I con- fess I al-ways will.

Yes, you are my fa- v'rite mem- o - ry.

No, I can't dis - miss your first hel - lo, your good-bye kiss.

Yes,_____ that day to me_____ will be my fa - v'rite mem - o - ry.

slowing ...... *ritard.*

Valse (♩ = ♪)
a tempo, gracefully

f

E7

Some

MY RIFLE, MY PONY AND ME

from the 1959 Motion Picture RIO BRAVO

Music by DIMITRI TIOMKIN
Words by PAUL FRANCIS WEBSTER

NEVER BE IT SAID

from the 1949 Motion Picture CHAMPION

Words and Music by DIMITRI TIOMKIN
and AARON GOLDMARK
Arranged Paul Henning

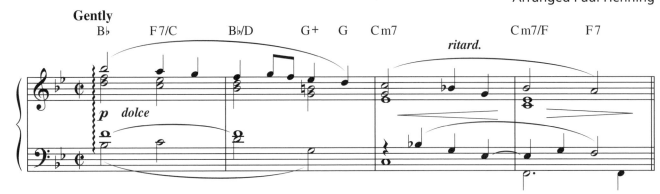

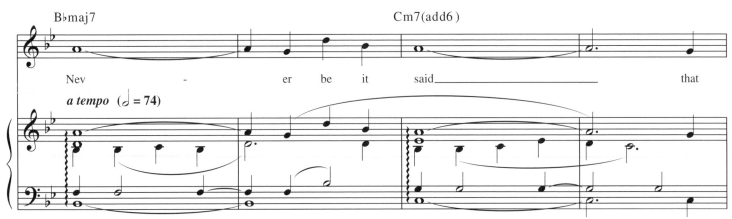

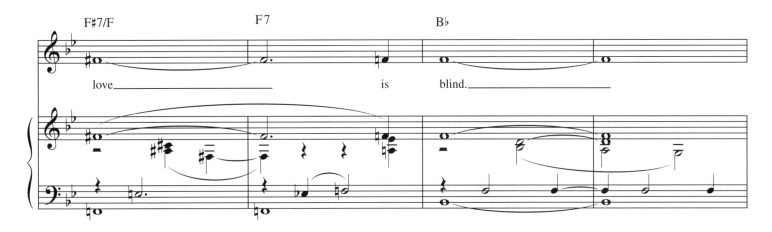

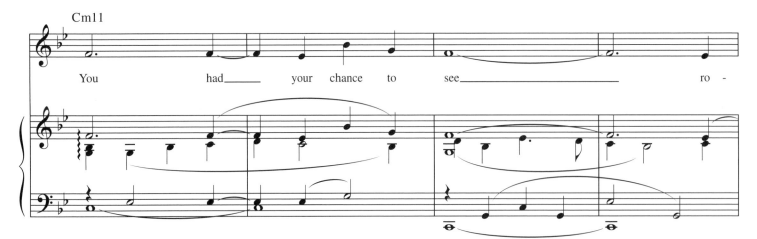

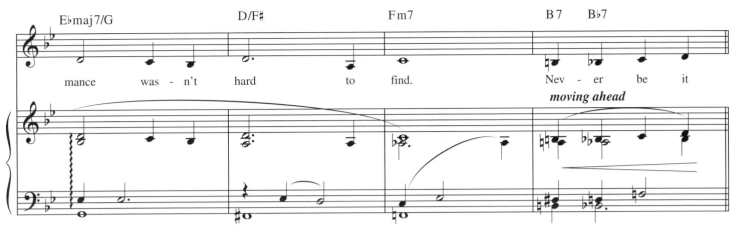

mance was -- n't hard to find. Nev -- er be it

moving ahead

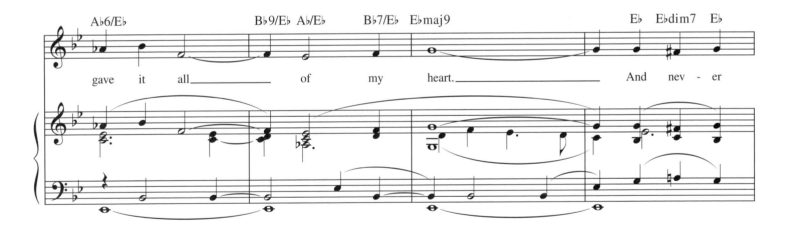

said that I_____ gave love a quick go by._____ In -- stead, I

poco più mosso

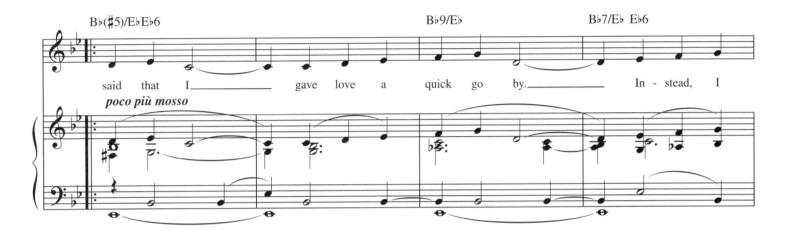

gave it all_____ of my heart._____ And nev -- er

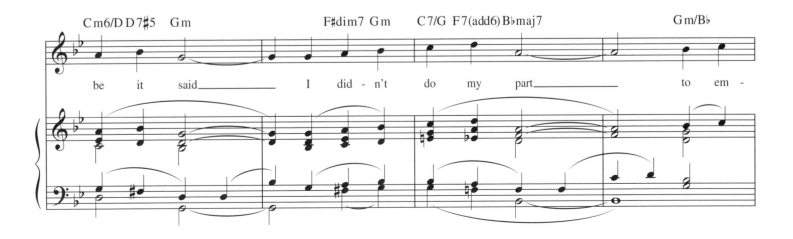

be it said_____ I did -- n't do my part_____ to em -

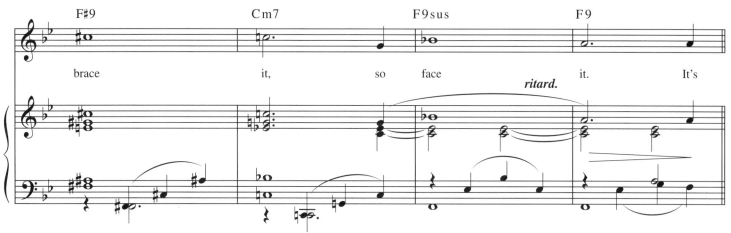

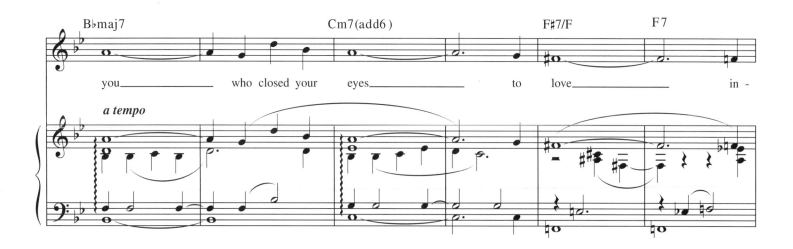

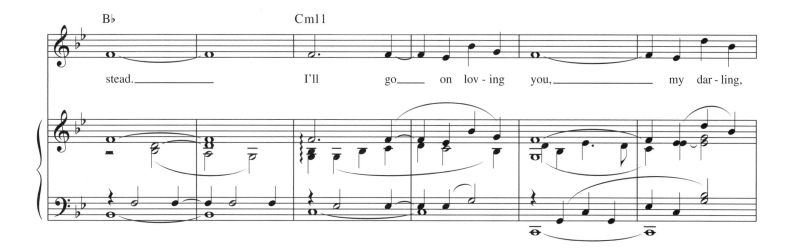

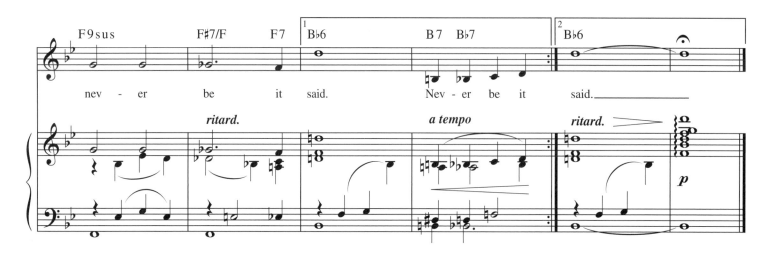

THE OLD MAN AND THE SEA

from the 1958 Motion Picture THE OLD MAN AND THE SEA

Music by DIMITRI TIOMKIN
Words by PAUL FRANCIS WEBSTER

NOSTALGIA
from the 1953 Motion Picture ANGEL FACE

By DIMITRI TIOMKIN

Con tristezza (♩ = 75 - 80)

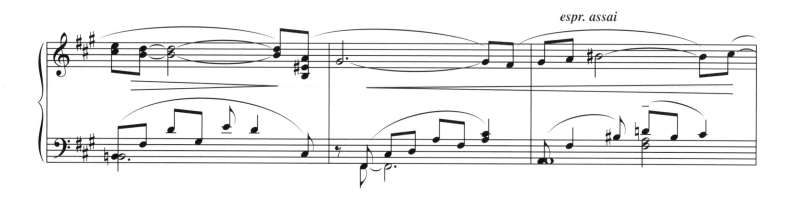

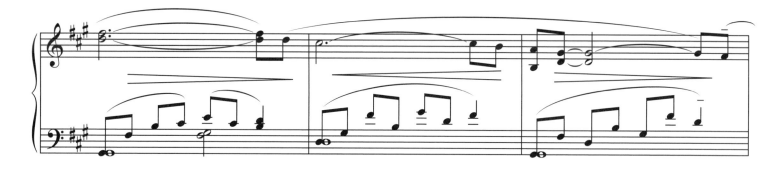

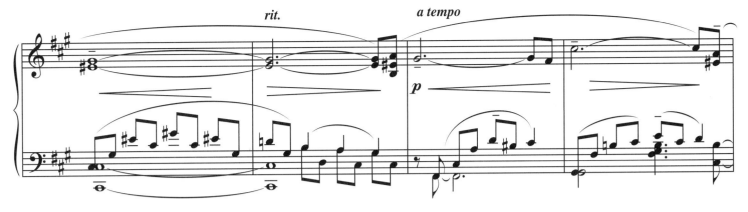

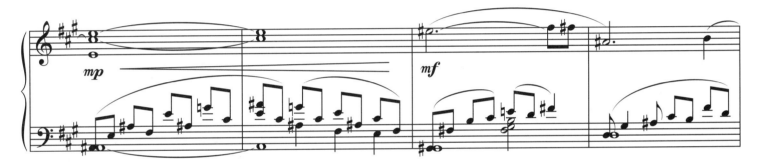

THE PEKING THEME
(So Little Time)
from the 1963 Motion Picture 55 DAYS AT PEKING

Words by PAUL FRANCIS WEBSTER
Music by DIMITRI TIOMKIN

Slowly, with expression (♩ = 72-76)

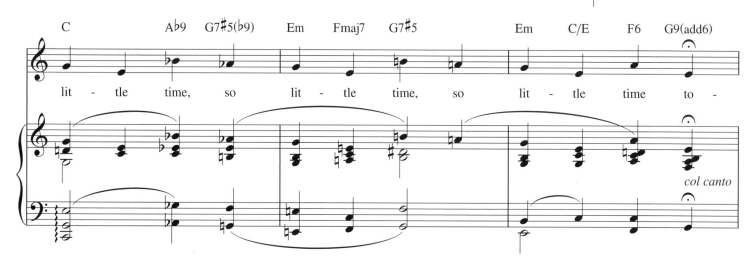

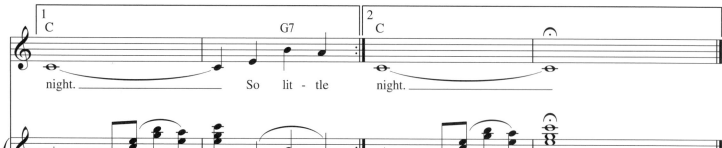

THE PRINCE AND PRINCESS WALTZ
(Grace Kelly Wedding Waltz)
for the 1956 wedding of Prince Rainier and Grace Kelly

Words by Ned Washington
Music by DIMITRI TIOMKIN
Arranged by Warren Sherk

Elegantly, in 3 (♩=140)

poco rit.

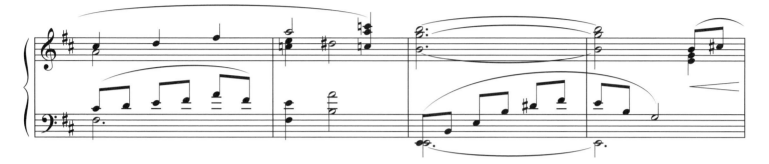

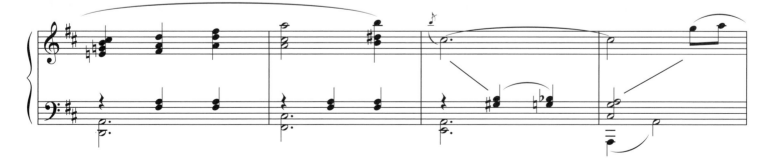

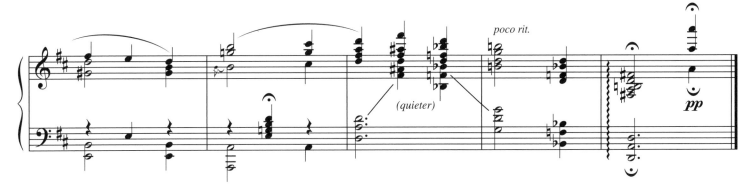

THE PRINCE AND PRINCESS WALTZ
(Grace Kelly Wedding Waltz)
for the 1956 wedding of Prince Rainier and Grace Kelly

Words by NED WASHINGTON
Music by DIMITRI TIOMKIN
Edited by Paul Henning

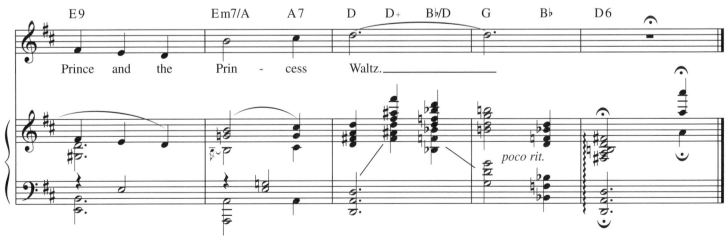

Original lyrics by Ned Washington for the occasion of the royal wedding:

All the world will be dancing, dancing in dreams to the Grace Kelly Wedding Waltz.
To the gay and entrancing melodious themes of the Grace Kelly Wedding Waltz.
Like the Prince and the Princess, let's dance through life, let us dance though the music halts.
Take your place, play your part on the throne in my heart; to the Grace Kelly Wedding Waltz.

QUAND JE RÊVE

from the 1952 Motion Picture THE BIG SKY

Music by DIMITRI TIOMKIN
Words by GORDON T. CLARK

Poco più mosso

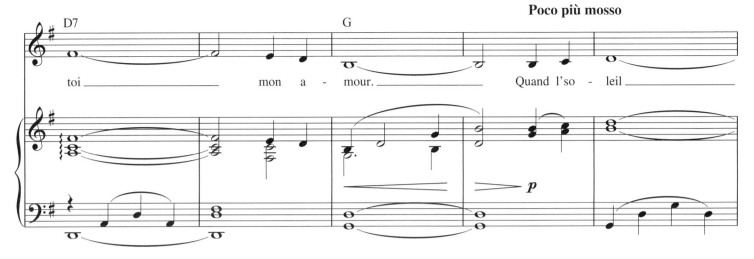

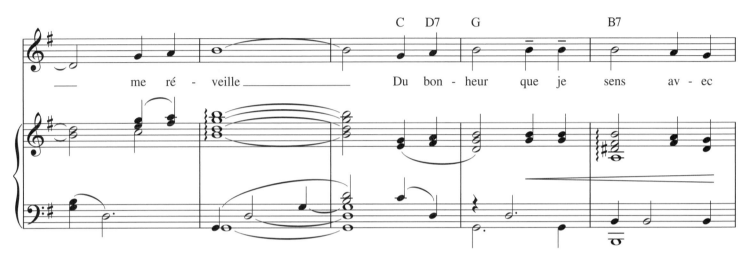

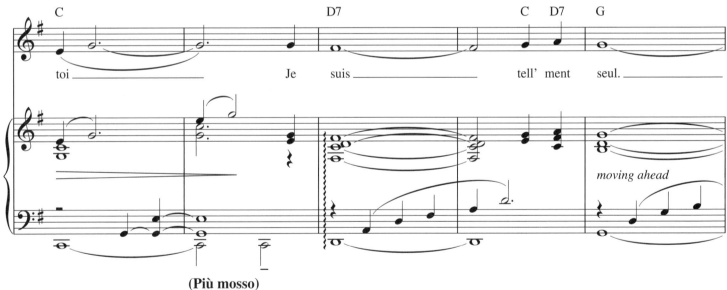

(Più mosso)

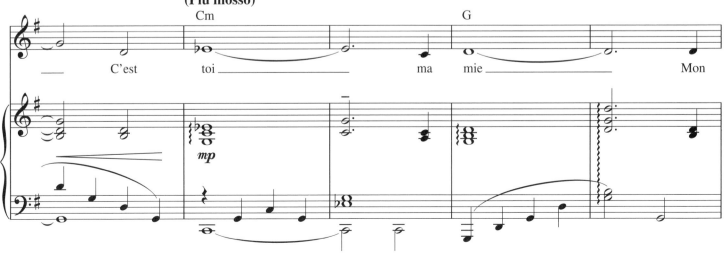

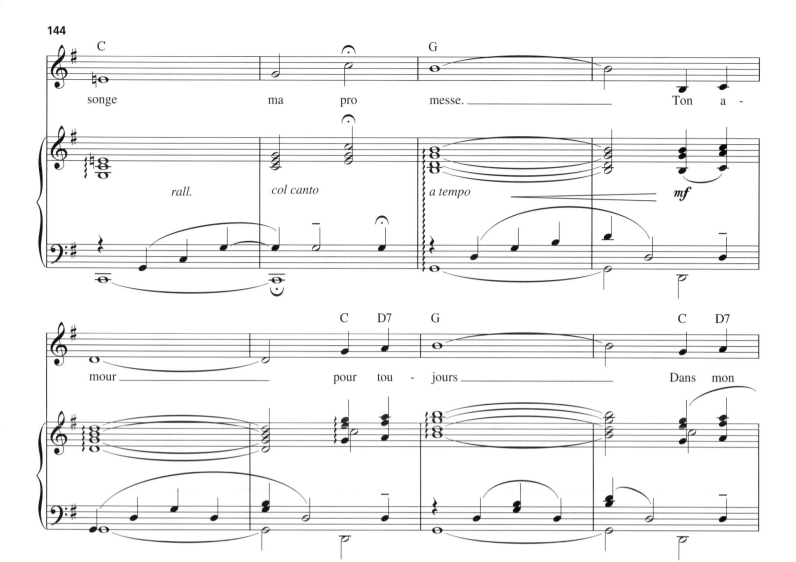

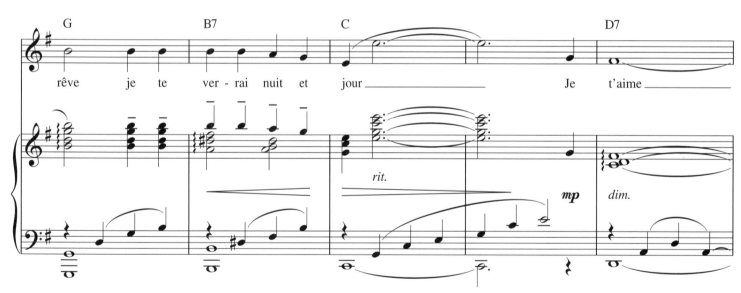

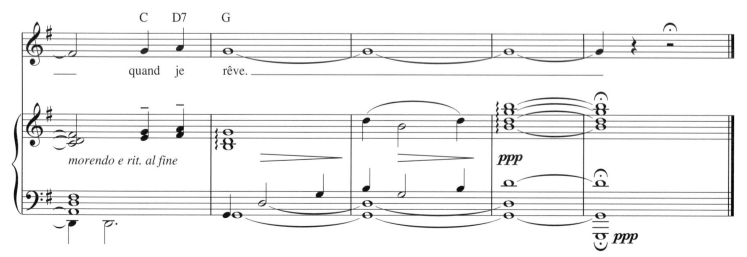

RETURN TO PARADISE

from the 1953 Motion Picture RETURN TO PARADISE

Words by NED WASHINGTON
Music by DIMITRI TIOMKIN

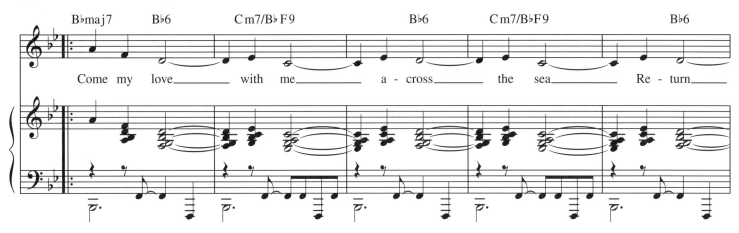

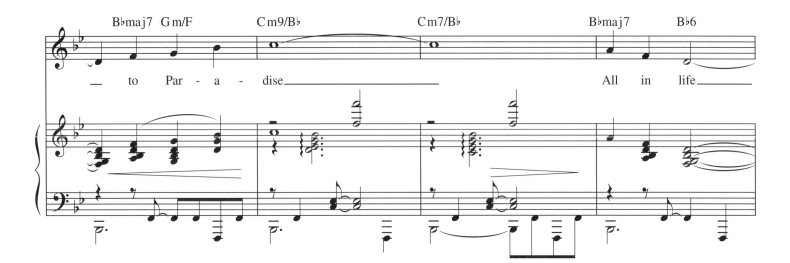

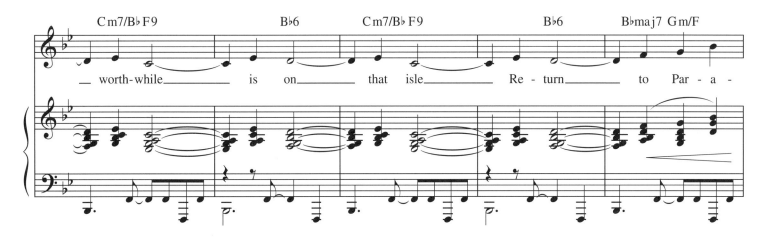

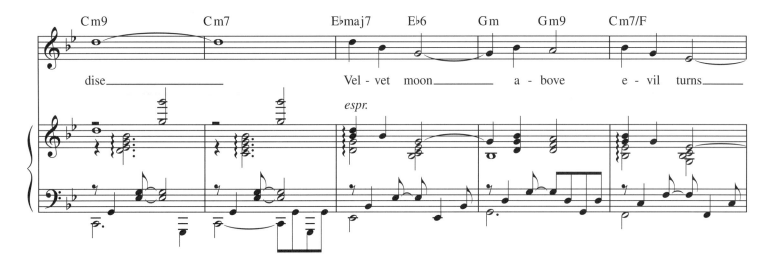

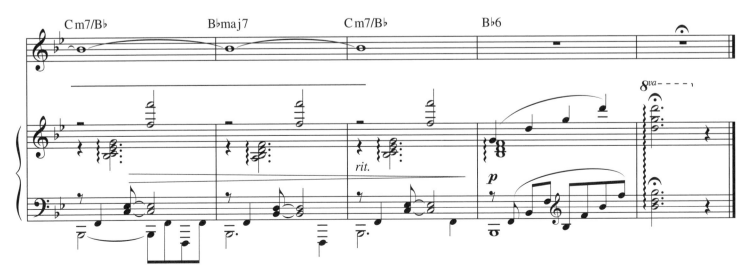

RAWHIDE

from the 1959 Television Series RAWHIDE

Words and Music by DIMITRI TIOMKIN
and NED WASHINGTON
Arranged by Patrick Russ

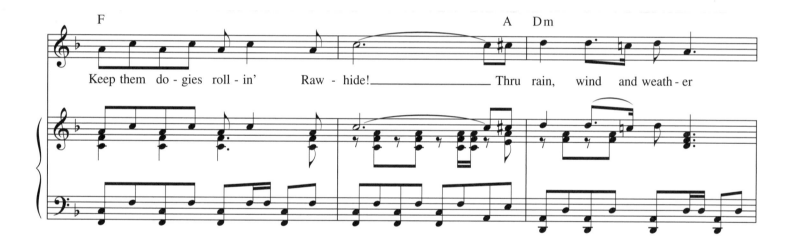

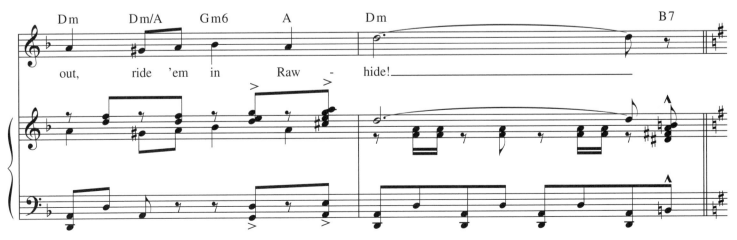

Mov-in', mov-in', mov-in', Though they're dis-ap-prov-in', Keep them do-gies mov-in' Raw-

hide! Don't try to un-der-stand 'em, Just rope and throw and brand 'em,

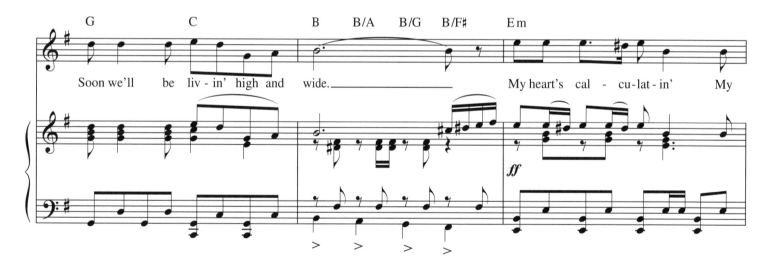

Soon we'll be liv-in' high and wide._____ My heart's cal-cu-lat-in' My

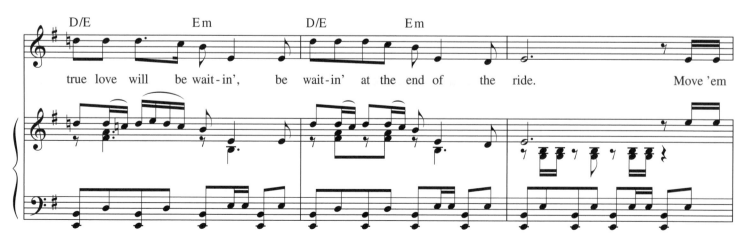

true love will be wait-in', be wait-in' at the end of the ride. Move 'em

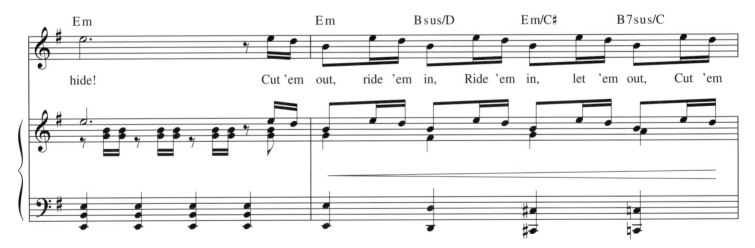

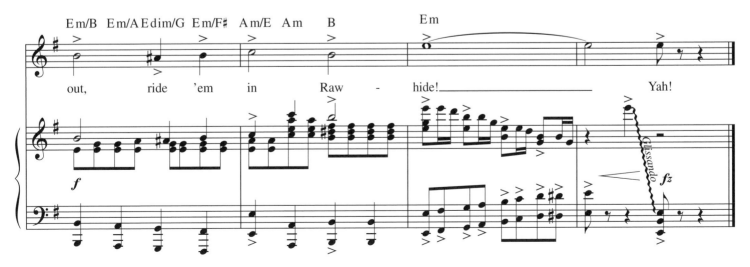

RIO BRAVO

from the 1959 Motion Picture RIO BRAVO

Music by DIMITRI TIOMKIN
Words by PAUL FRANCIS WEBSTER

Moderately (♩ = c. 80)

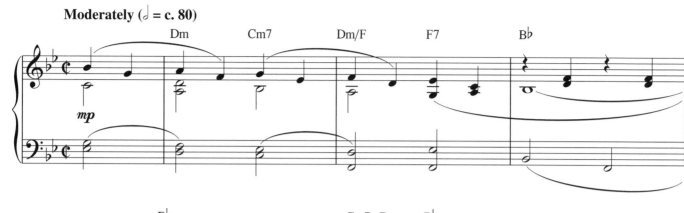

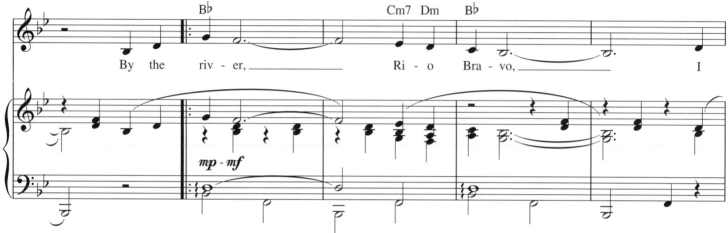

By the riv - er, _____ Ri - o Bra - vo, _____ I

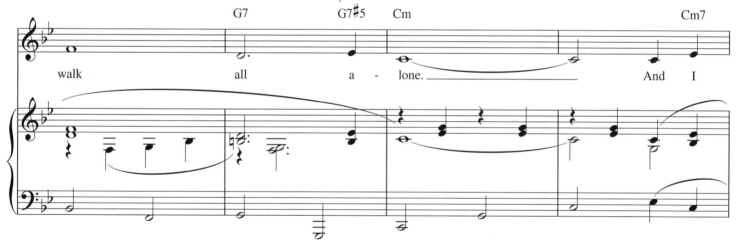

walk all a - lone. _____ And I

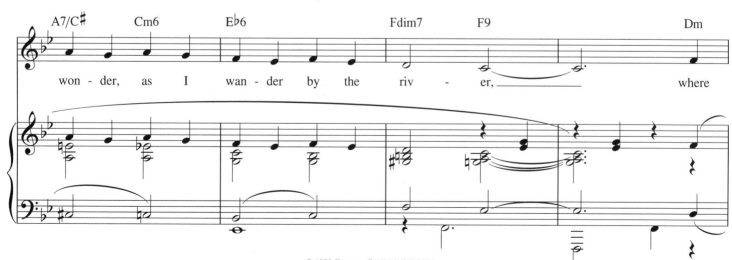

won - der, as I wan - der by the riv - er, _____ where

ROCKETTE SONG

from the 1950 unproduced Stage Musical THE BIG TIME REVUE

Lyrics by ARNOLD HEWITT
Music by DIMITRI TIOMKIN
Edited by Paul Henning

THE SUNDOWNERS

from the 1960 Motion Picture THE SUNDOWNERS

By DIMITRI TIOMKIN
Arranged by Patrick Russ

A tempo, poco meno (♩ = 72)

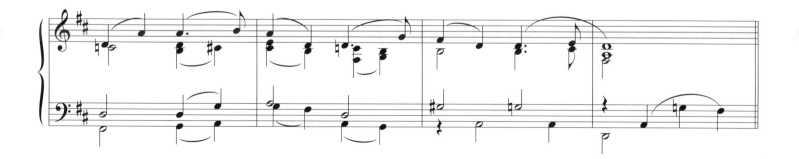

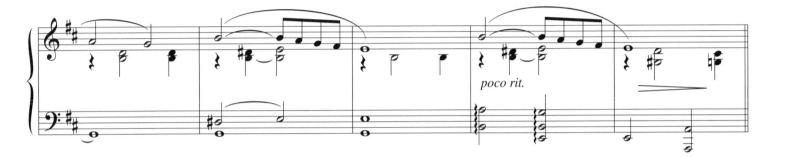

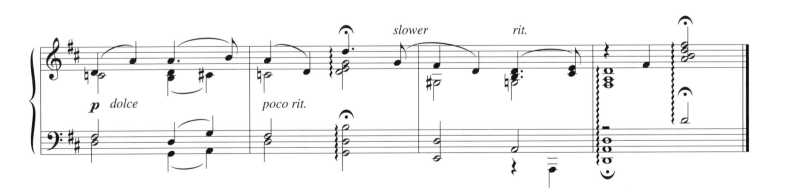

STRANGE ARE THE WAYS OF LOVE

from the 1959 Motion Picture THE YOUNG LAND

Words by NED WASHINGTON
Music by DIMITRI TIOMKIN

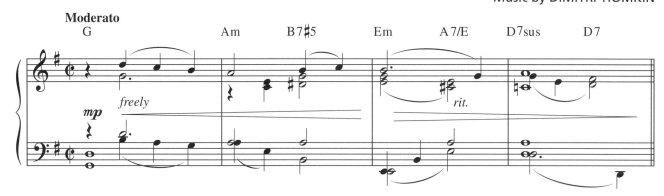

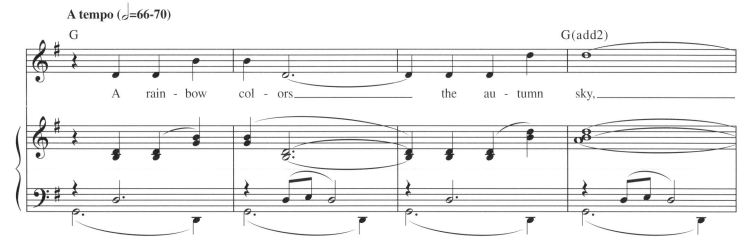

A rain-bow col-ors the au-tumn sky,

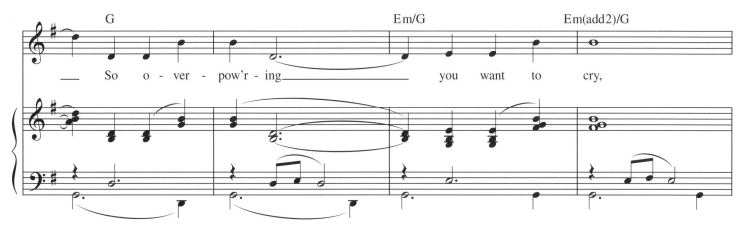

So o-ver-pow'r-ing you want to cry,

Yet no one sees it, but you and I, Strange are the

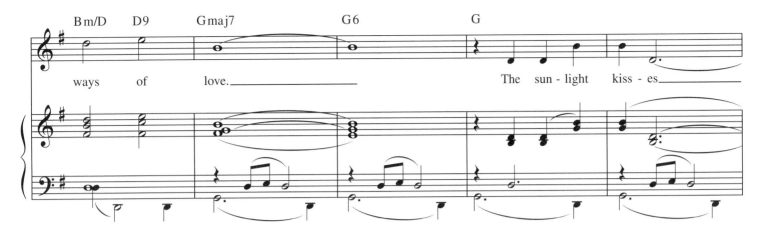

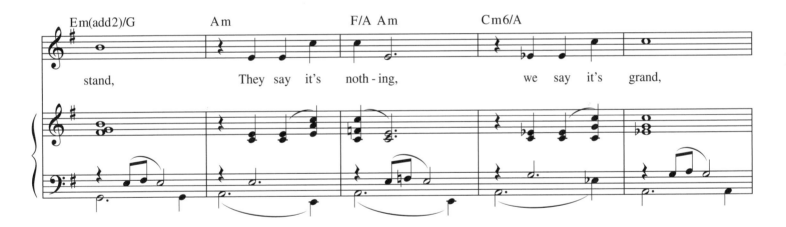

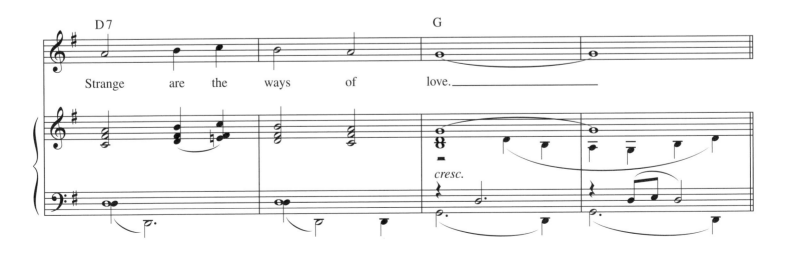

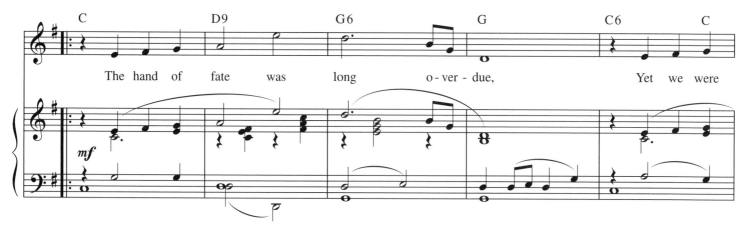

The hand of fate was long o-ver-due, Yet we were

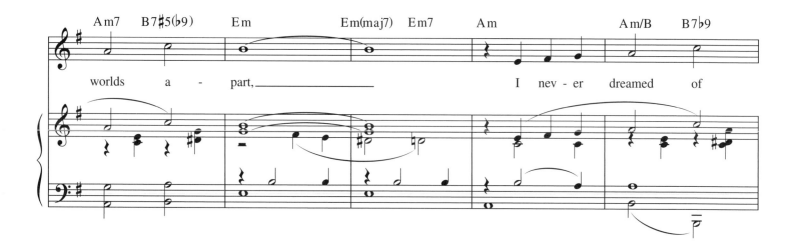

worlds a - part,_____ I nev - er dreamed of

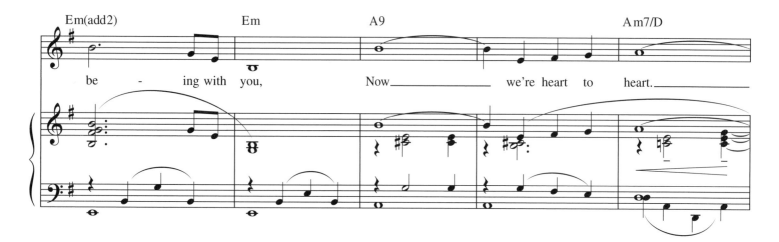

be - ing with you, Now_____ we're heart to heart._____

— This is a young land_____ and young are we,_____

_ We know how ten-der_____ young love can be, But in my

rap-ture it seems to me, Strange are the ways of

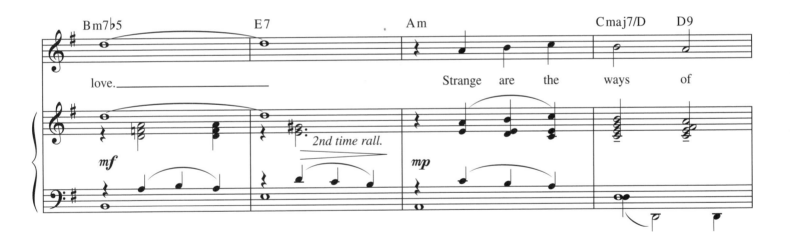

love._____ Strange are the ways of

love._____ love._____

STRANGE LADY IN TOWN

from the 1955 Picture STRANGE LADY IN TOWN

Music by DIMITRI TIOMKIN
Words by NED WASHINGTON
Arranged by Paul Henning

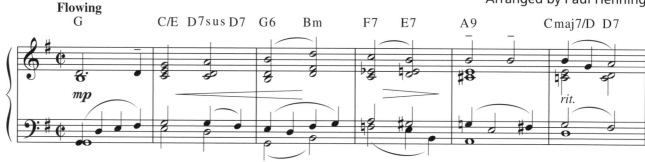

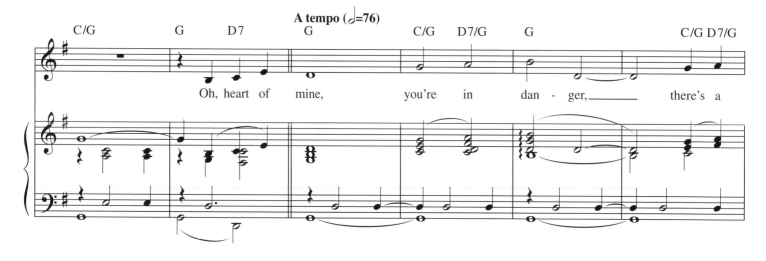

Oh, heart of mine, you're in dan-ger,_____ there's a

strange la-dy in town._____ Who is this heart steal-in'

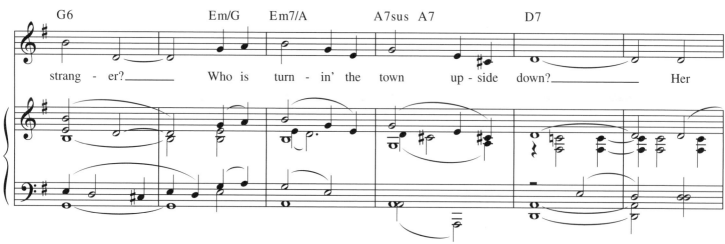

strang-er?_____ Who is turn-in' the town up-side down?_____ Her

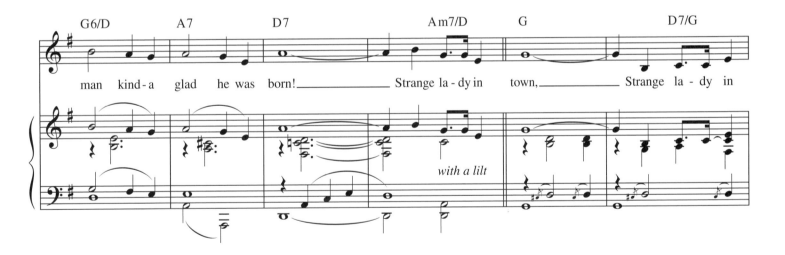

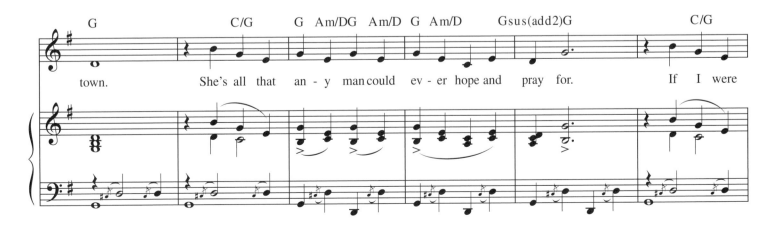

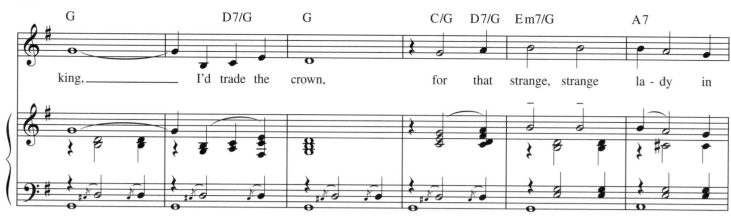

king,_____ I'd trade the crown, for that strange, strange la - dy in

town!_____ Ain't got no ring for her fin - ger,_____ and I

can't buy her a gown._____ But rain or shine, I'll still

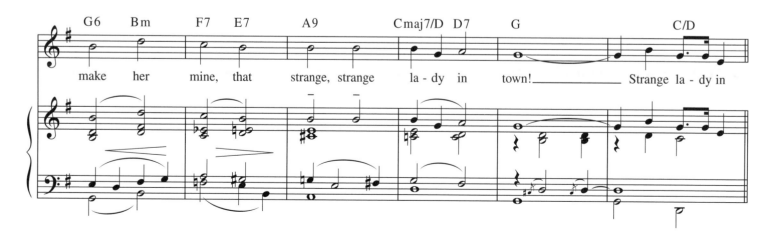

make her mine, that strange, strange la - dy in town!_____ Strange la - dy in

town,_____ Strange la - dy in town,_____ She's all that an - y man could ev - er hope and

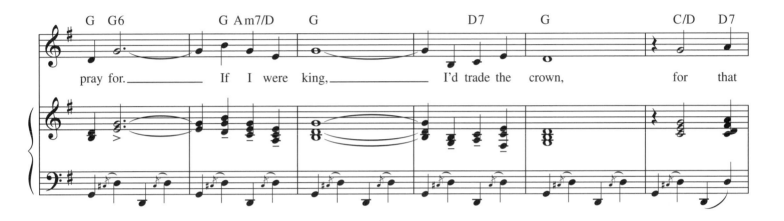

pray for._____ If I were king,_____ I'd trade the crown, for that

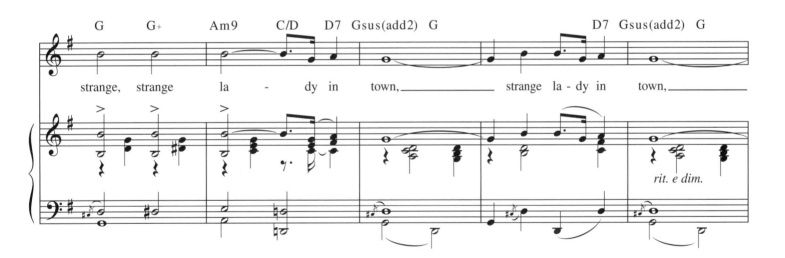

strange, strange la - dy in town,_____ strange la - dy in town,_____

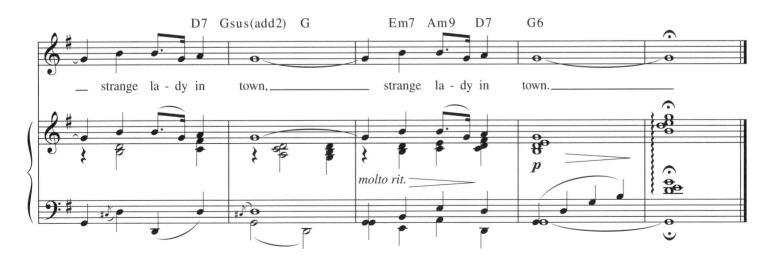

_ strange la - dy in town,_____ strange la - dy in town._____

SWEET SURRENDER

from the 1943 unproduced Stage Musical SWEET SURRENDER

Words by FREDERICK HERBERT
Music by DIMITRI TIOMKIN
Edited by Paul Henning

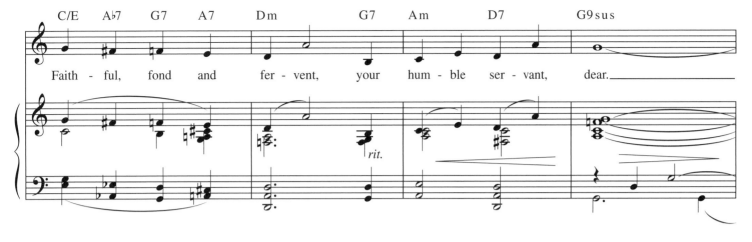

Faithful, fond and fervent, your humble servant, dear.

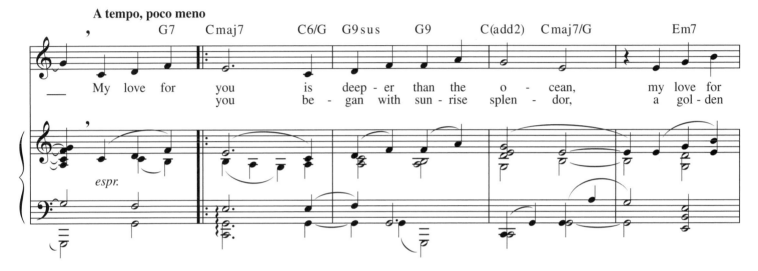

A tempo, poco meno

My love for you is deeper than the ocean, my love for
you began with sunrise splendor, a golden

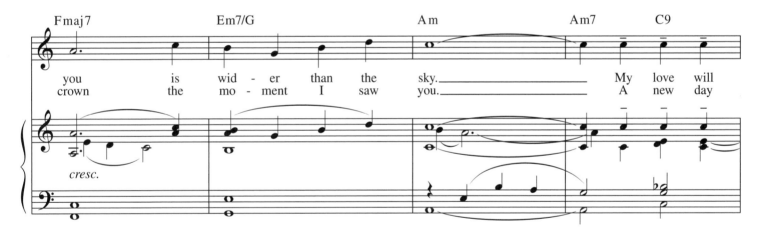

you is wider than the sky. My love will
crown the moment I saw you. A new day

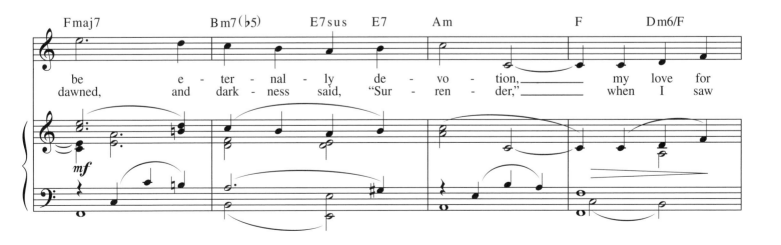

be eternally devotion, my love for
dawned, and darkness said, "Surrender," when I saw

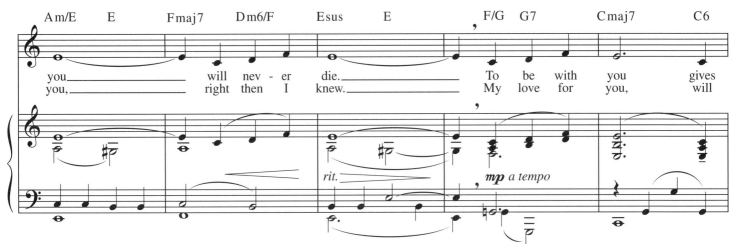

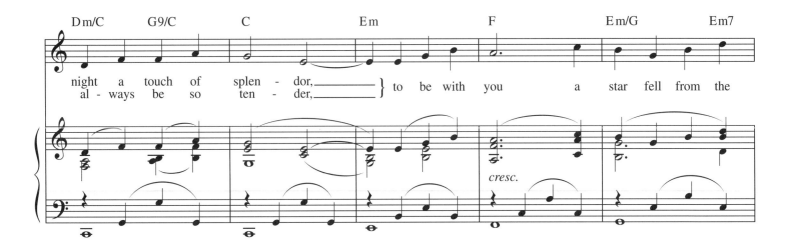

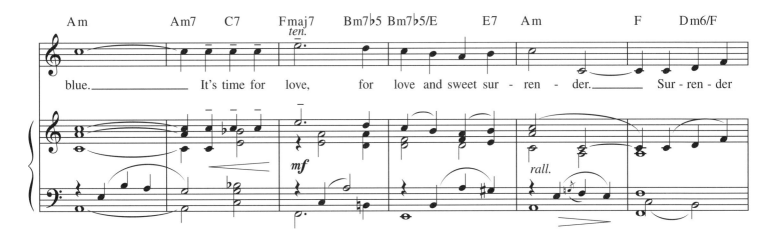

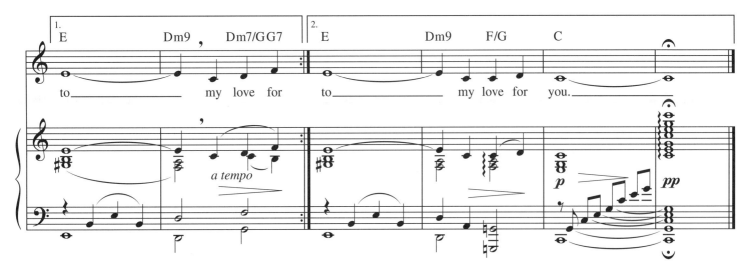

THEME FROM "36 HOURS"
(A Heart Must Learn to Cry)
from the 1965 Motion Picture 36 HOURS

Music by DIMITRI TIOMKIN
Words by PAUL FRANCIS WEBSTER

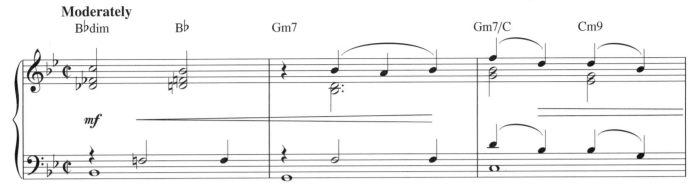

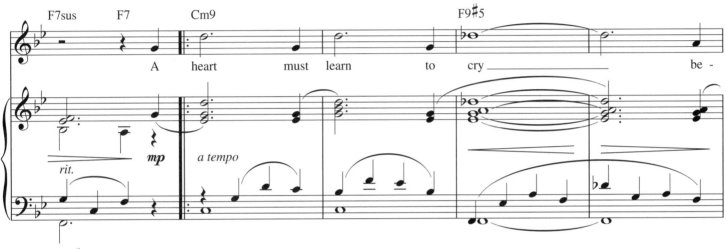

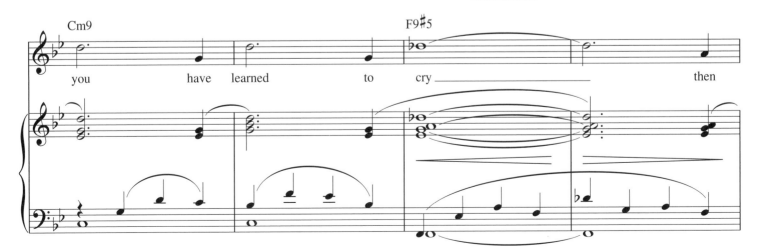

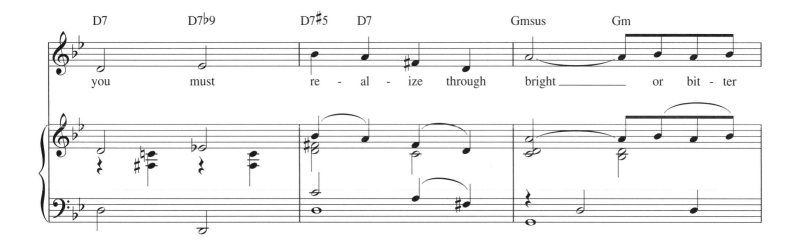

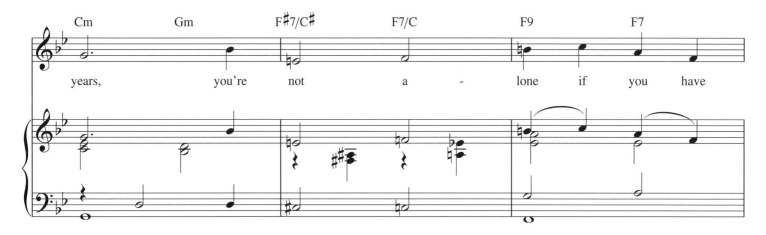

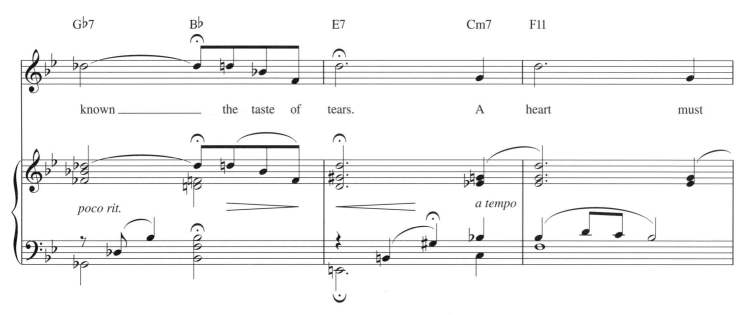

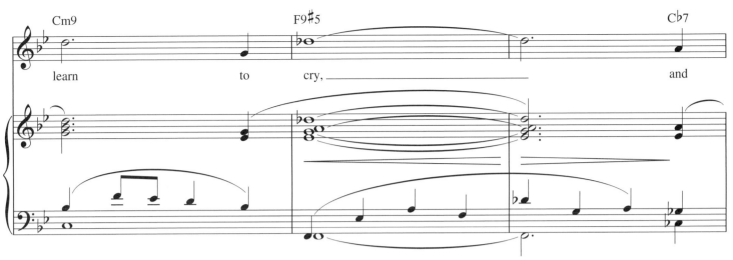

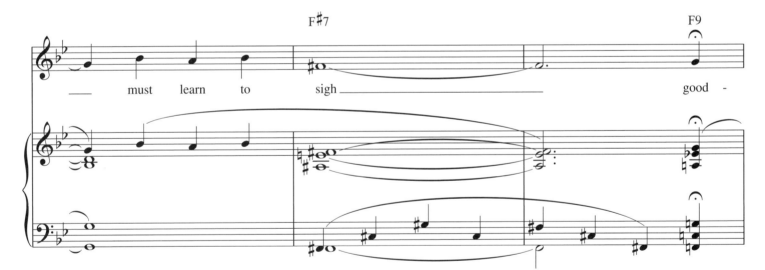

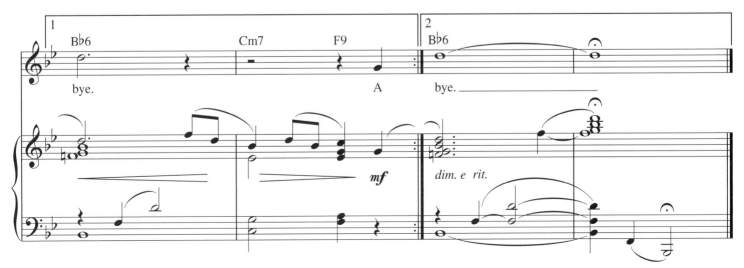

TOWN WITHOUT PITY

from the 1961 Motion Picture TOWN WITHOUT PITY

Words and Music by DIMITRI TIOMKIN
and NED WASHINGTON

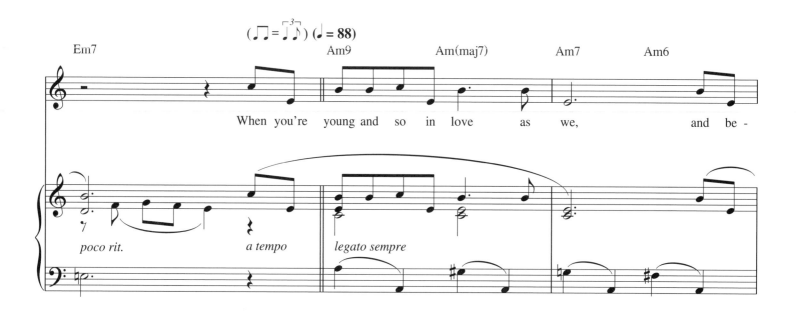

When you're young and so in love as we, and be-

wil- dered by the world we see, _____ why do peo- ple hurt us so, on- ly

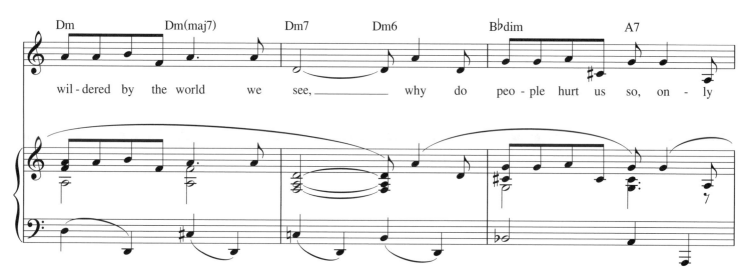

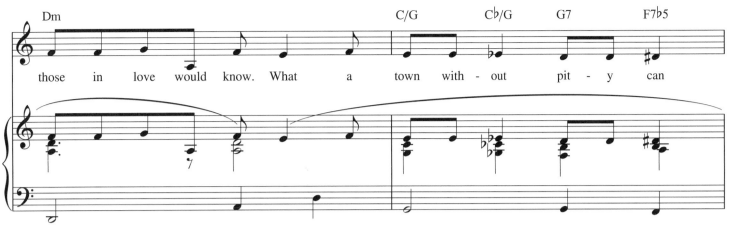

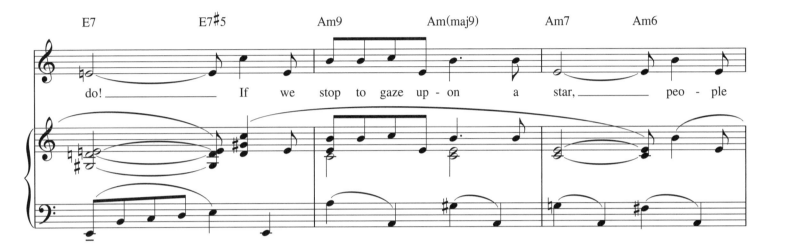

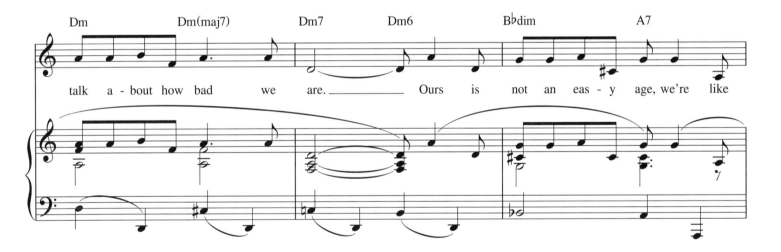

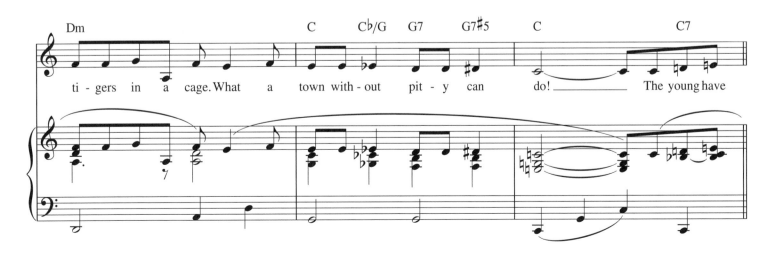

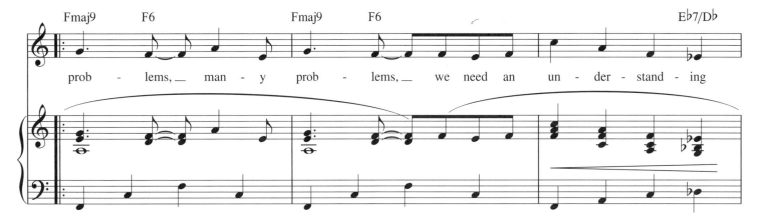

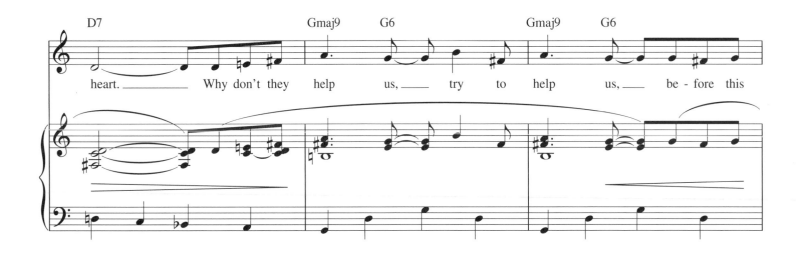

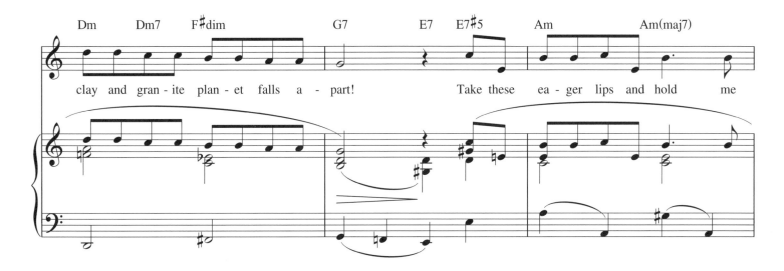

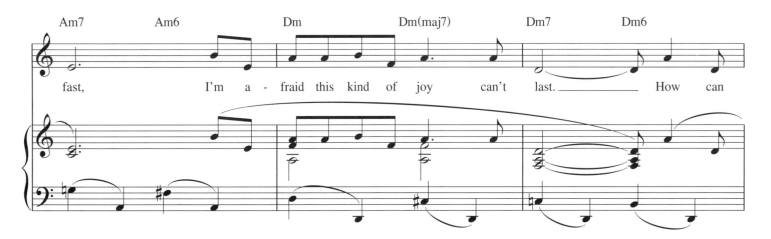

WAIT FOR LOVE

from the 1956 Motion Picture TENSION AT TABLE ROCK

Words by NED WASHINGTON
Music by DIMITRI TIOMKIN

WILD IS THE WIND

from the 1957 Motion Picture WILD IS THE WIND

Words by NED WASHINGTON
Music by DIMITRI TIOMKIN

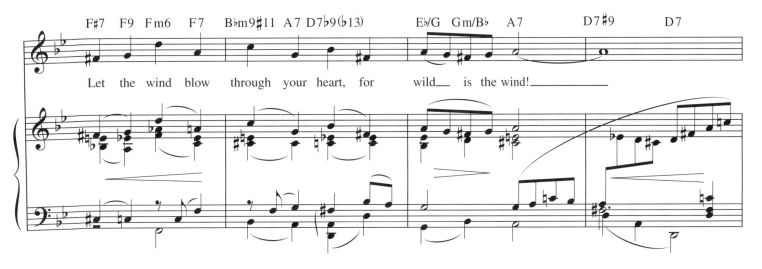

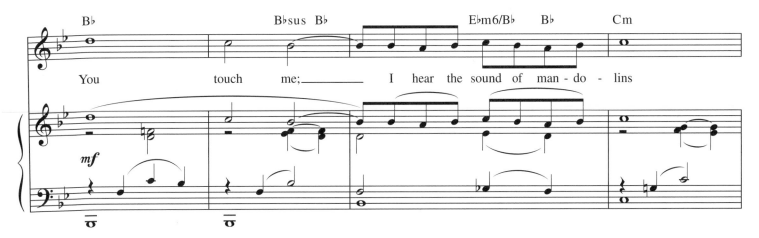

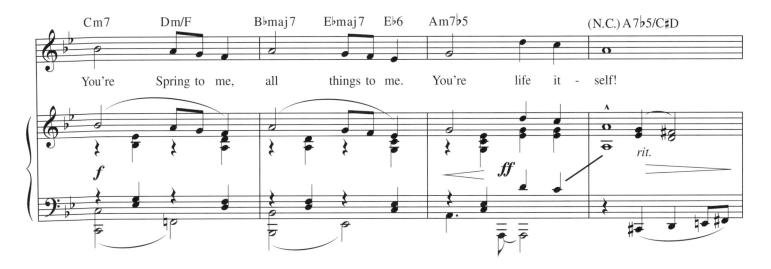